Scott Grimando's The Art of the Mythical Woman™

www.theArtoftheMyth.com

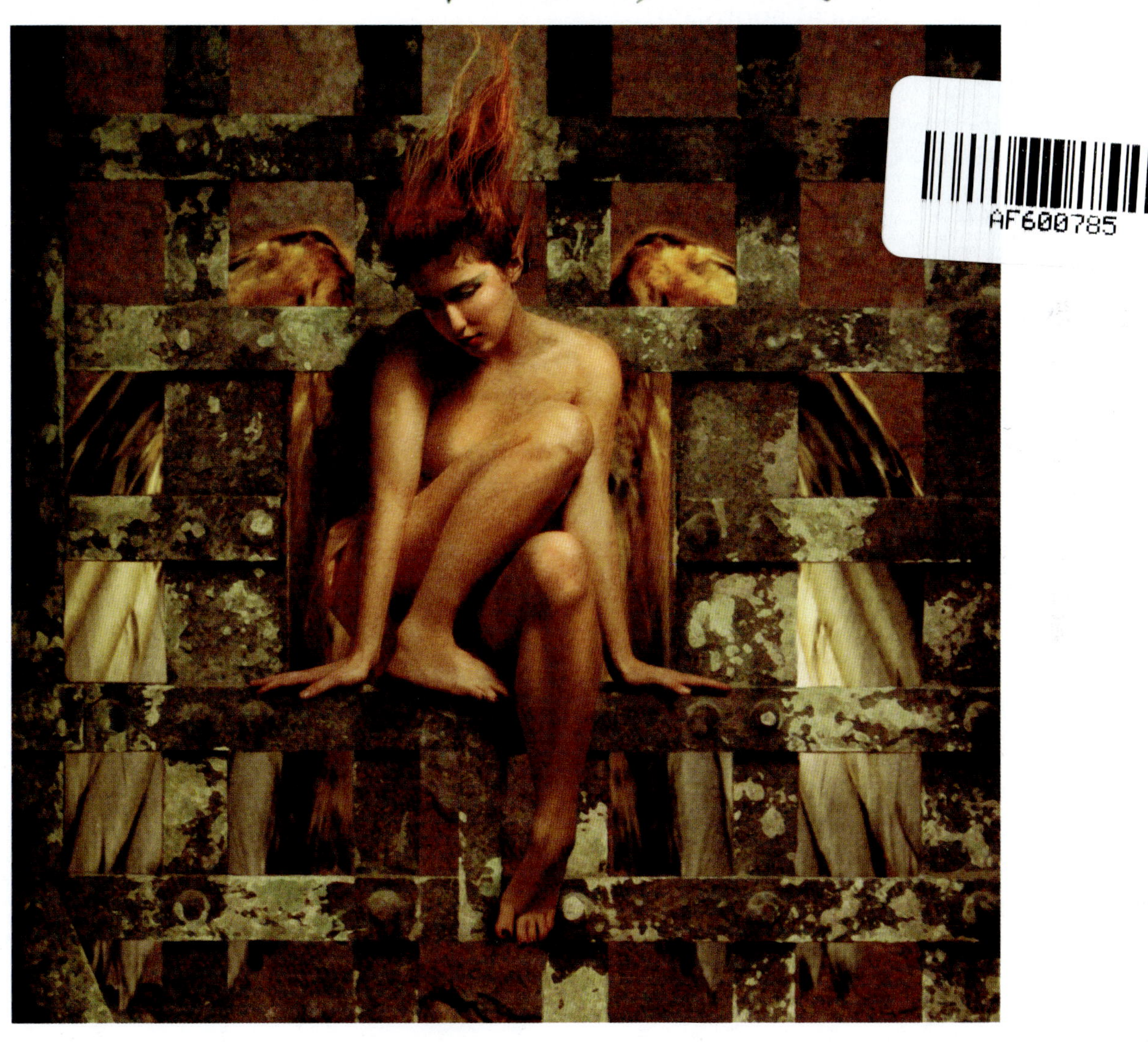

Lucid Dreams

Artist's Introduction

Covers and Commissions: The first part of this book explores some of my best book covers and magazine commissions. I'll give you an overview of what goes into fulfilling an assignment.
From concept sketch to completion, the illustrator must find a way to create his own design aesthetic. I strive to blur the line between fine art and illustration because I don't think there should be a distinction between the two. I've always wanted to create art that spoke to people, to tell a story through a visual narrative.
The study of classical painters reveals that they were illustrators telling mythical stories to amuse the public or taking commissions to pay their bills and refine their craft. I believe that art is created for the viewer not the artist.
My first mentor, Harold Stevenson, was one of the few students of Norman Rockwell and I'm proud to carry on the grand tradition of the traditional painting techniques he taught me. However, an artist can't overlook the tools at his disposal so I integrate the computer into my creative process while striving to maintain a classical approach.

Personal Work: The second part of this book features some of my personal visions. Much of my private work, my Lucid Dreams, revolves around my passion for the female form. The body of work is called "The Art of the Mythical Woman" but I explore many of our modern mythologies. Spaceflight, alien cultures, robotics, these are our modern myths. What's fascinating about modern fiction is that it all seems within our grasp today. The world has transformed itself within my lifetime in terms of science and technology but I can't help but notice how humanity has stayed the same. Our hopes and fears, our passions and desires are timeless. Through the application of traditional painting skills and digital illustration techniques I hope to achieve something just as timeless.
As in the first part of the book, I'll outline the ideas and techniques used.

Scott Grimando's
The Art of the Mythical Woman
Volume One Lucid Dreams
Artwork Text & Layout

Dedicated to my loving wife Pamela

Published by SQP Inc
PO Box 248 - Columbus, NJ 08022

Sal Quartuccio & Bob Keenan - Publishers

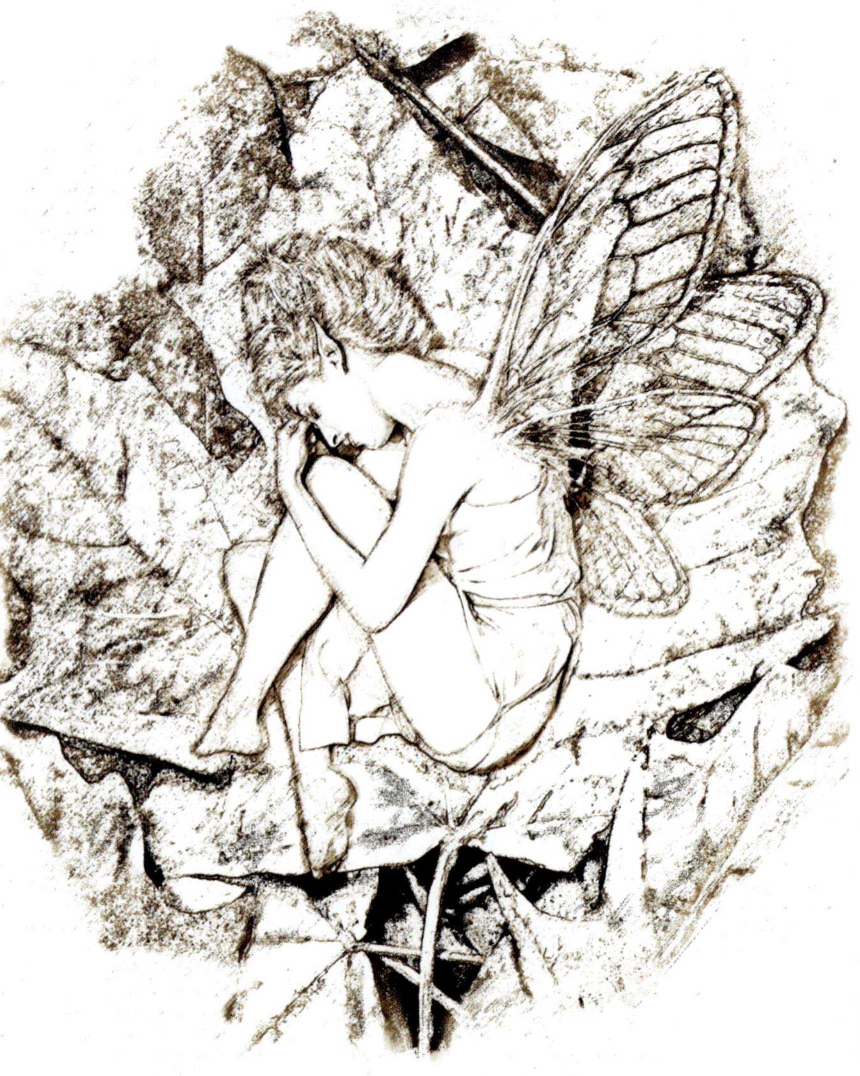

To the right: Crushed Autumn Sketch for Faerie Magazine Cover

Opposite page: The Green Sword Inquest Magazine Spread
Digital: Photoshop/Painter

Front Cover: Islands (detail)
Digital: Photoshop/Painter

Introduction

Scott Grimando is deeply dedicated to his artistic passions. An initial glance at his images gleams a thoughtful and deliberate approach to his craft – masterful and intense research of his figures, exploration of dynamic compositions and lighting, and development of compelling narratives. Weaving these elements together pulls the characters of his futuristic and fantasy worlds into that of our own. His landscapes are those you and I might wander down and inhabit with light streaming through trees and leaves gathering beneath your footsteps, all very familiar but for the fairy reclining upon the rock by the stream. We are convincingly transported to another time and place through the masterful realism Scott brings to his work.

Dedication is an easy word to place forward as the explanation to why these images are so successful. The depths and refinement of skill needed to weave these illusions cannot be fully appreciated until you understand the lengths to which this artist has grappled with various pictorial problems, wrestled with them, and tamed their properties for his command of imaginary realism. The anatomy found within both passenger and mount in 'Dragon Rider' is an excellent example of the challenges Scott must undertake to perfect his craft. The placement of a convincing figure upon the dragon's back requires careful staging of the figure model, references, costumes, and overall body language to simulate such an experience. He then couples her with the construct of the dragon: realistic anatomical bone structure, wing design, skin pattern, and overall lighting unify and bring solidity to an entirely fabricated and imaginary creature. And that is but one part of the whole. Add atmospheric effects, from hazing to cloud formations, sensitivity to detail and light mass, awareness of architectural design and precision of perspective to integrate the dragon with the rest of its environment. He considers elements of composition and narrative to polish the forms: the sublime sweep of the tail and inclusion of another dragon. Finally, the artist must balance color, intensity of hue, and contrast to set up a graphically beautiful image both compelling and exciting to view. It is a wonder that such art is even possible, and even greater wonder that Scott is able to pull it off again and again. And again.

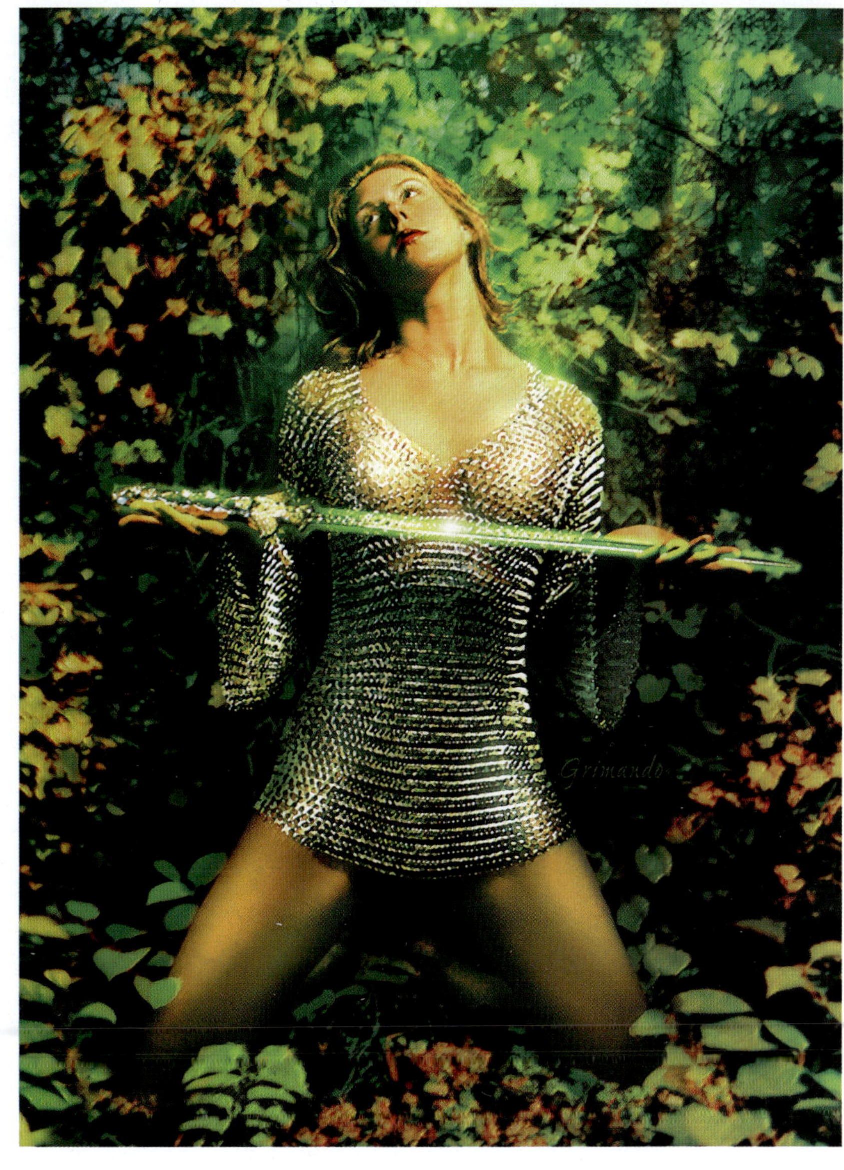

Every year I am amazed and thrilled at Scott's imagery and look forward to discover what precious worlds lie waiting for the rest of us to explore.

Donato Giancola

Channeling Cleopatra

Book Cover
Digital: Photoshop/Illustrator/Painter

This is one of my first book covers for Ace. I've since had a long relationship with the Art Director, Judy Murello. I find her to be a pleasure to work with. That's a rarity in this business.

Judy and I began the process by discussing various ideas that the editors wanted to see. They were fixated on the popular Tomb Raider movie that had just come out. After reading the manuscript I realized that the story was much more spiritual then that. I discussed my idea with Judy and she liked it so I put together a rough very similar to what you see here. Unfortunately I also had to come up with something along the lines of what the editors wanted to see. A standard Tomb Raider girl walking into a tomb. Fortunately they liked my concept better and the cover came out great.

For the second book in the series, Cleopatra 7.2, we continued the theme. The sketch below was rejected because it wasn't similar enough to the first book. If a third book is written I'm not sure how I'm going to make the cover look original while maintaining the established theme.

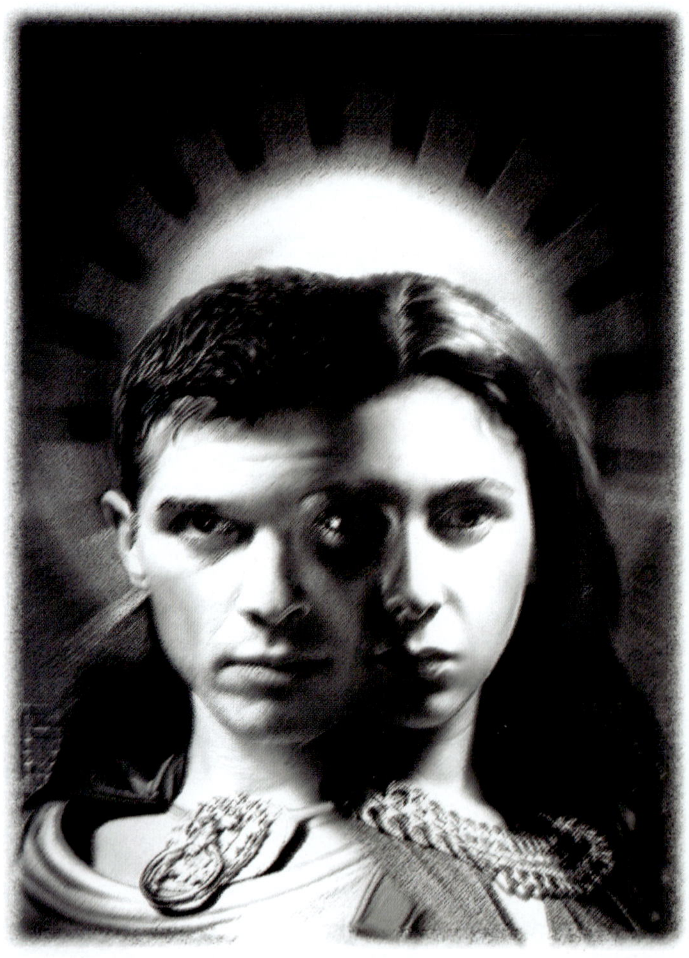

Cleopatra 7.2
Book Cover
Digital: Photoshop/Painter

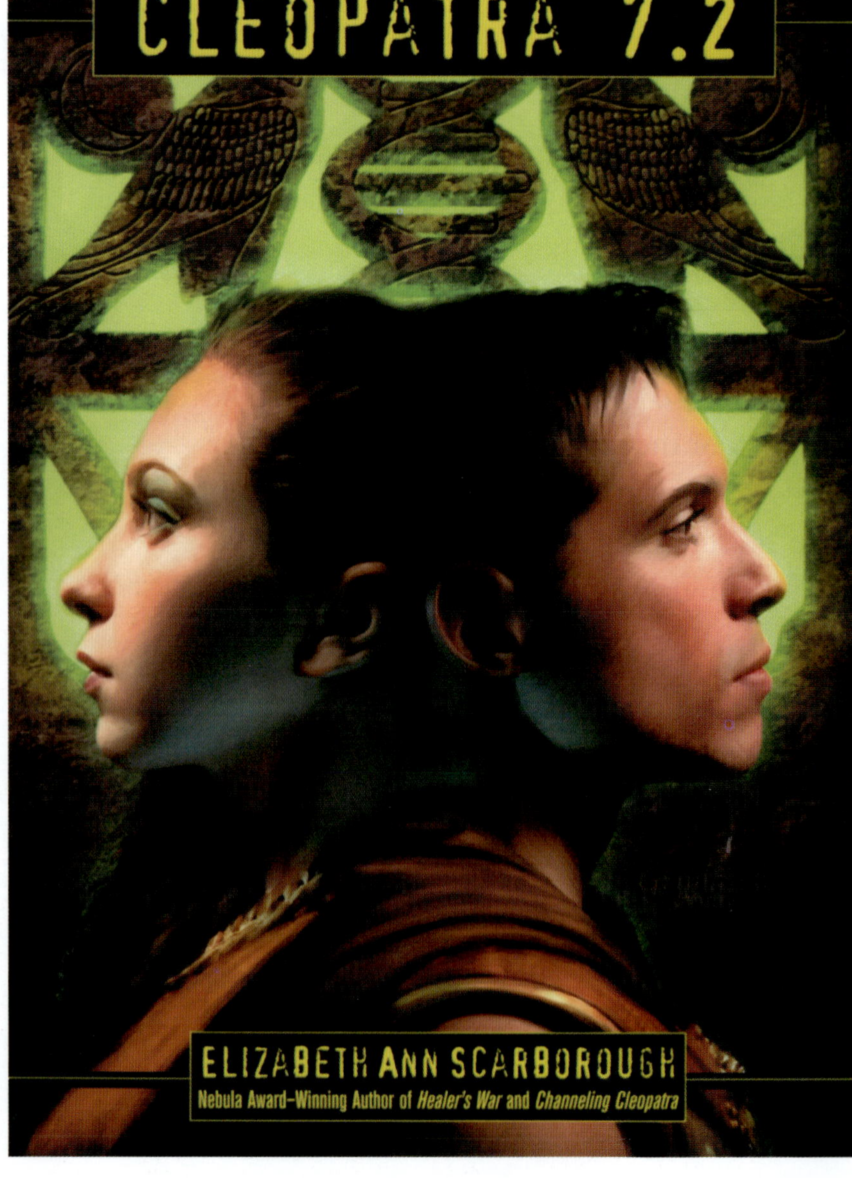

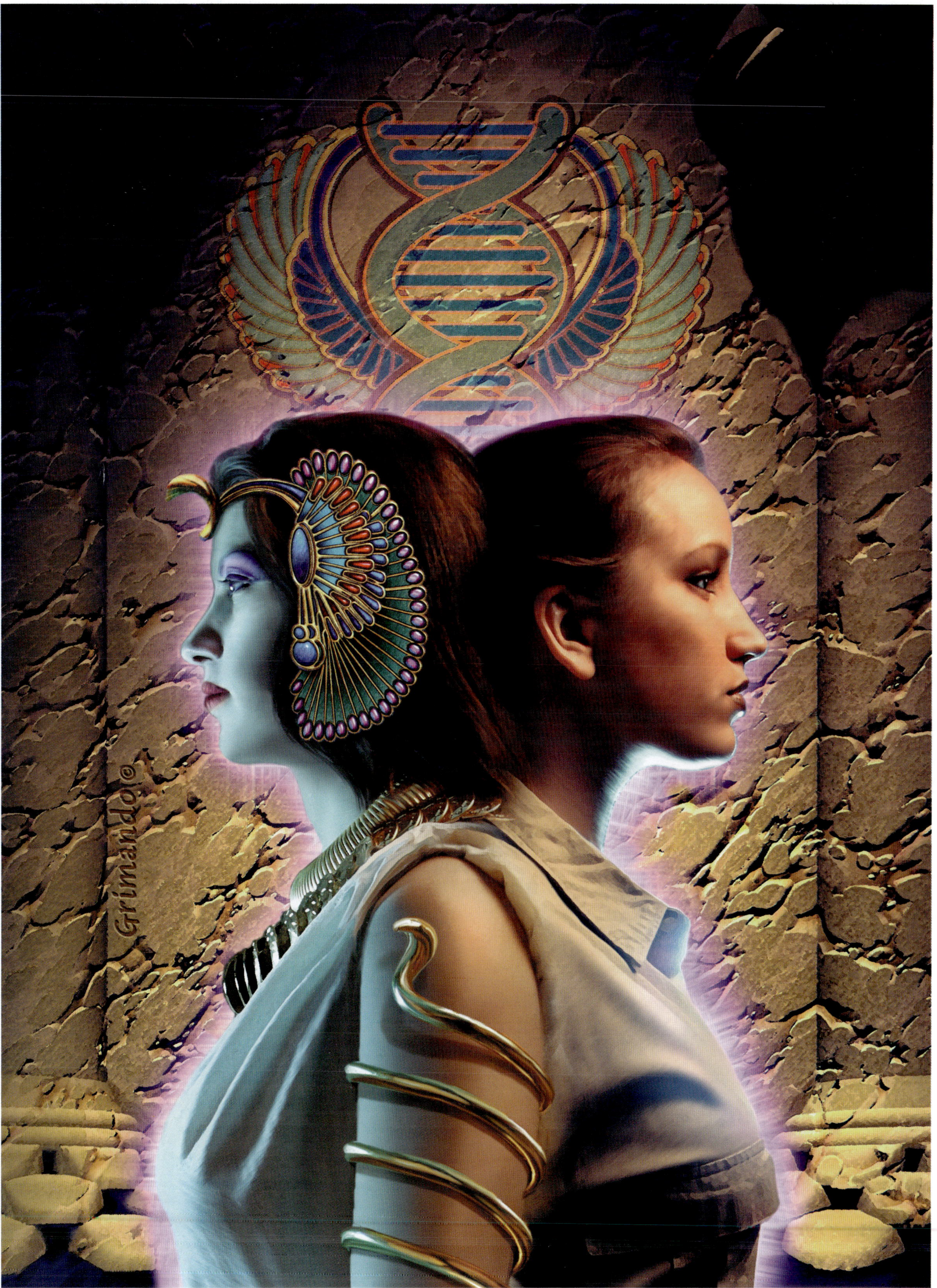
Grimando©

Kris Longknife Book 1: Mutineer

Book Cover
Digital: Photoshop/Painter/3D

One thing that's changed since I began working with computers is my interest in space ship design. With 3D programs I can sculpt anything I can imagine.

The Longknife series gives me the opportunity to explore space stations, battle ships, shuttles, and command centers in a far distant future.

The first step is to read through the manuscript looking for visual descriptions and important elements of the story. When I think I have the feel for it I begin looking for a model and designing costumes.

A close friend happened to match the description of the main character so I didn't have to search for her through local modeling agencies.

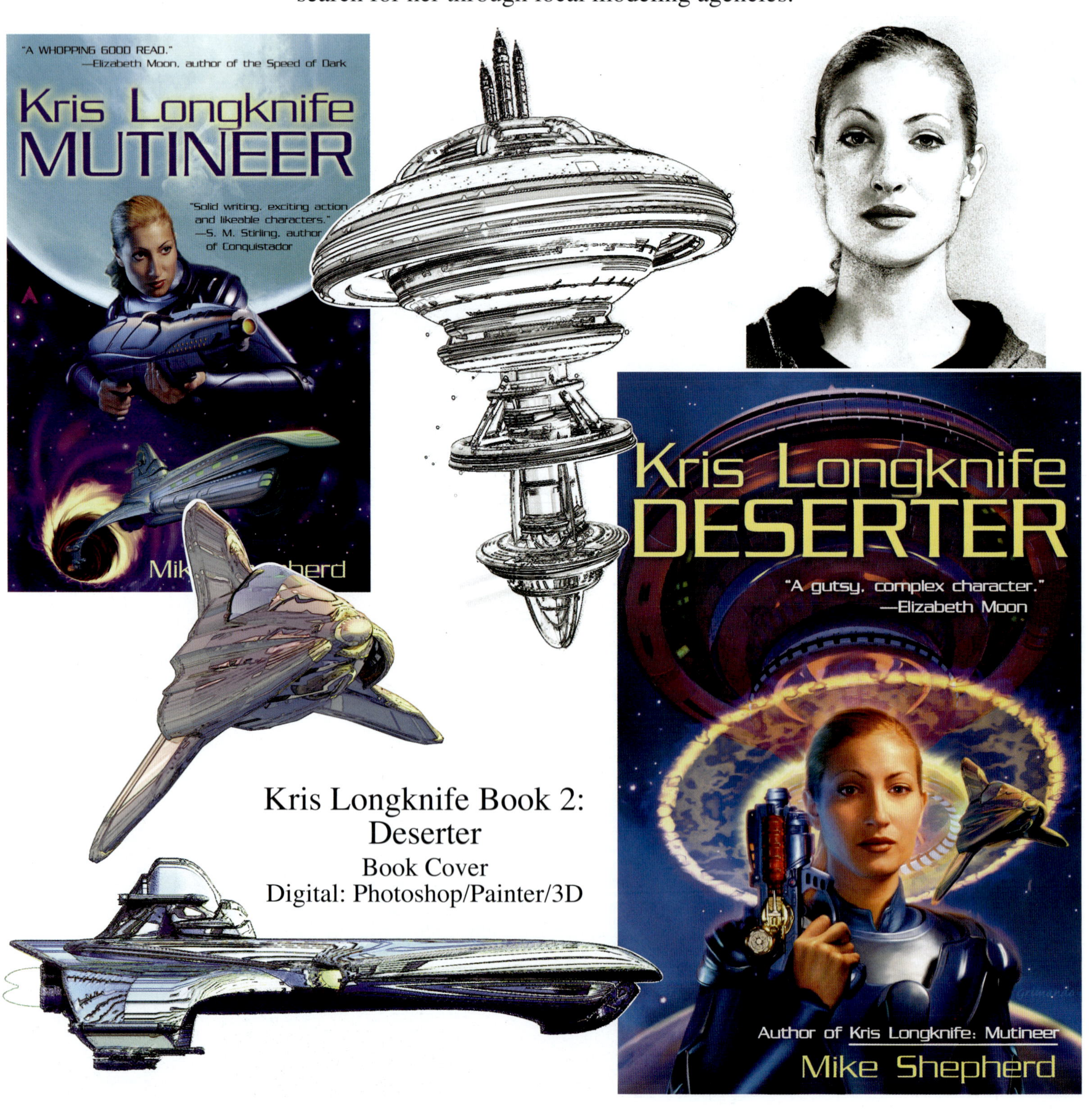

Kris Longknife Book 2: Deserter
Book Cover
Digital: Photoshop/Painter/3D

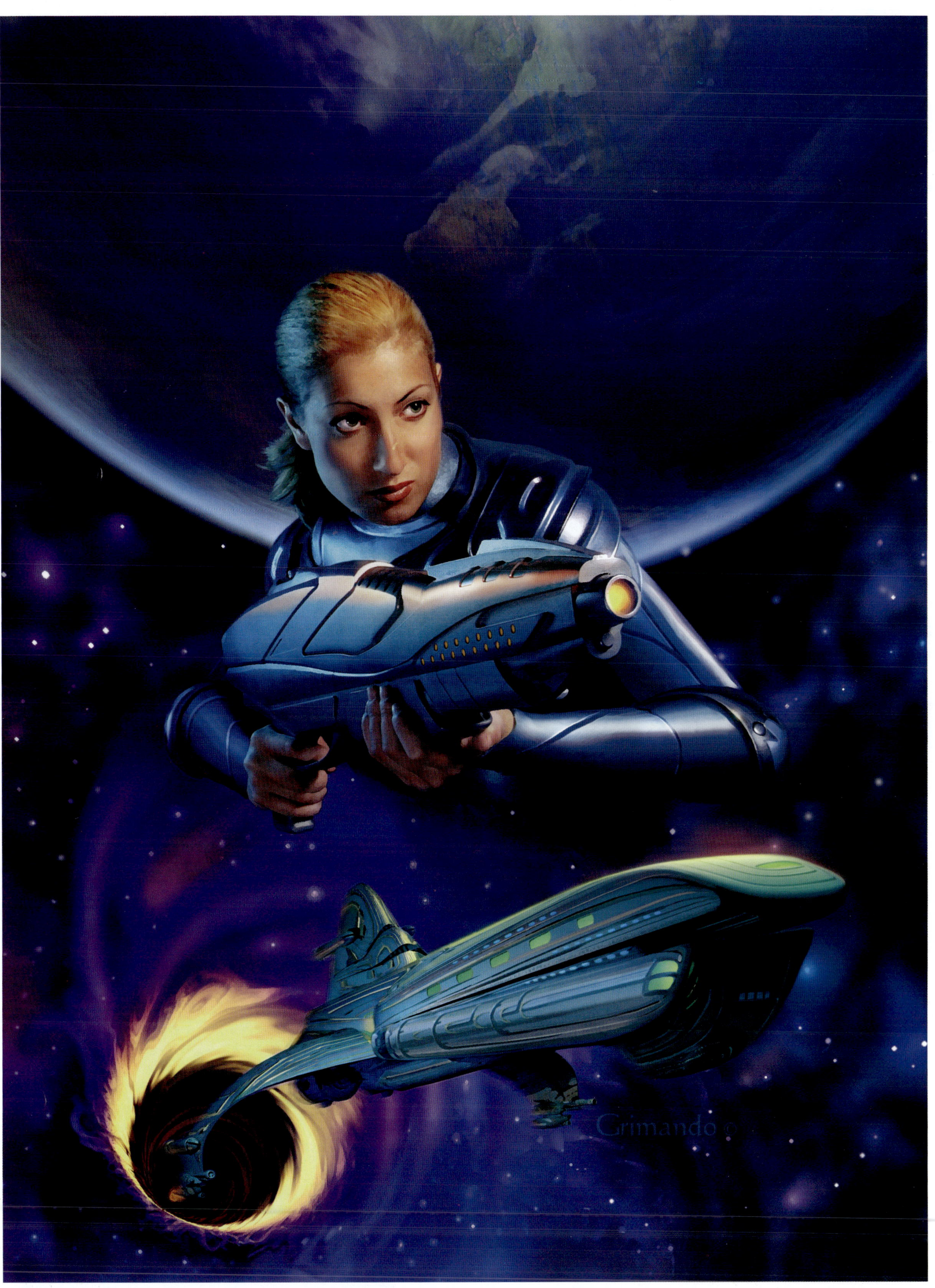
Grimando ©

Kris Longknife Book 3: Defiant

Book Cover
Digital: Photoshop/Painter/3D

The writer, Mike Shepherd, says very little about the actual look of the hardware in his manuscripts so I'm pretty much given free reign over the look of the ships and costume. After putting together several small color roughs and presenting them to the art director (Judy Murello) we decide on a design style that will carry through the series.
Then I piece together costumes from anything I can find and spray paint everything a metallic blue to match. A neoprene dive suit was painstakingly hand painted with metallic fabric paint, pieces of my boat were used and several sport paddings were disassembled and recombined. I really just want to create a costume that will give me a good base for the photo shoot. Afterwards I repaint everything in Photoshop and Painter.
Throughout the series I had to vary color schemes while maintaining the same design aesthetic.

The ships usually start out as rough sketches before I model them in 3D.

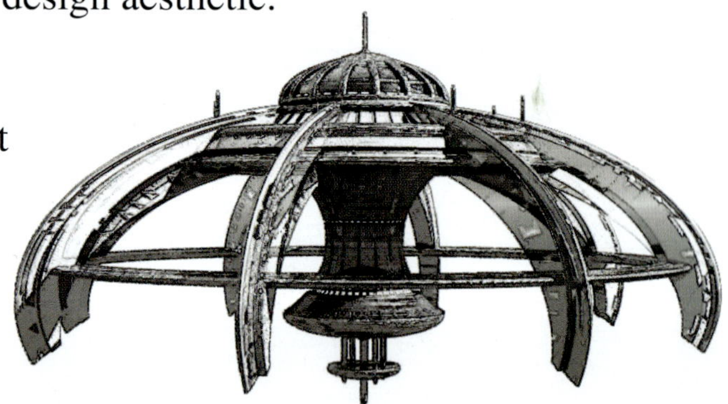

Kris Longknife Book 4: Resolute

Book Cover
Digital: Photoshop/Painter/3D

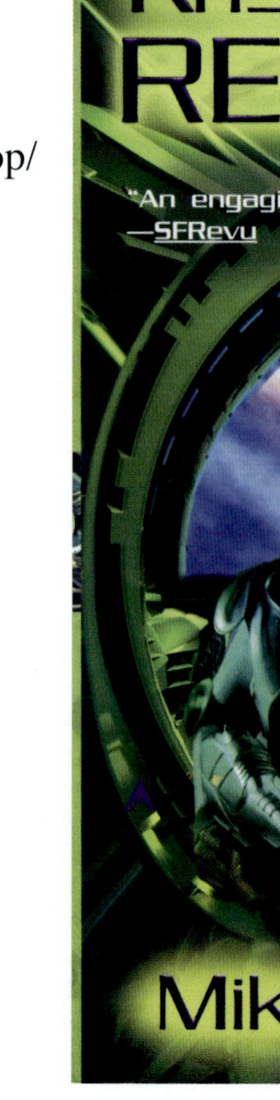

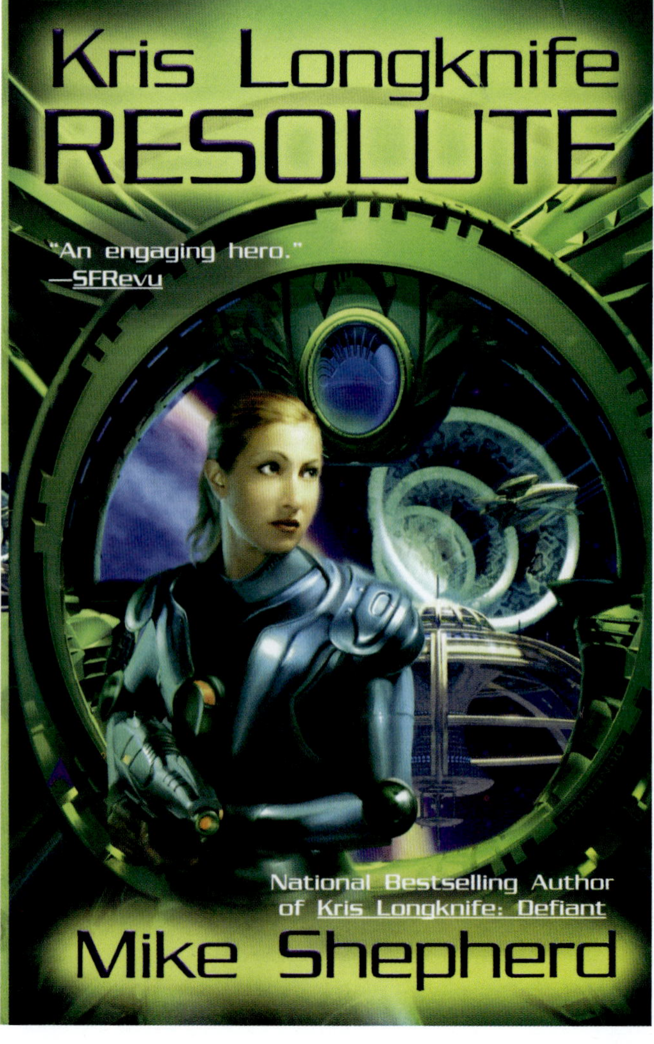

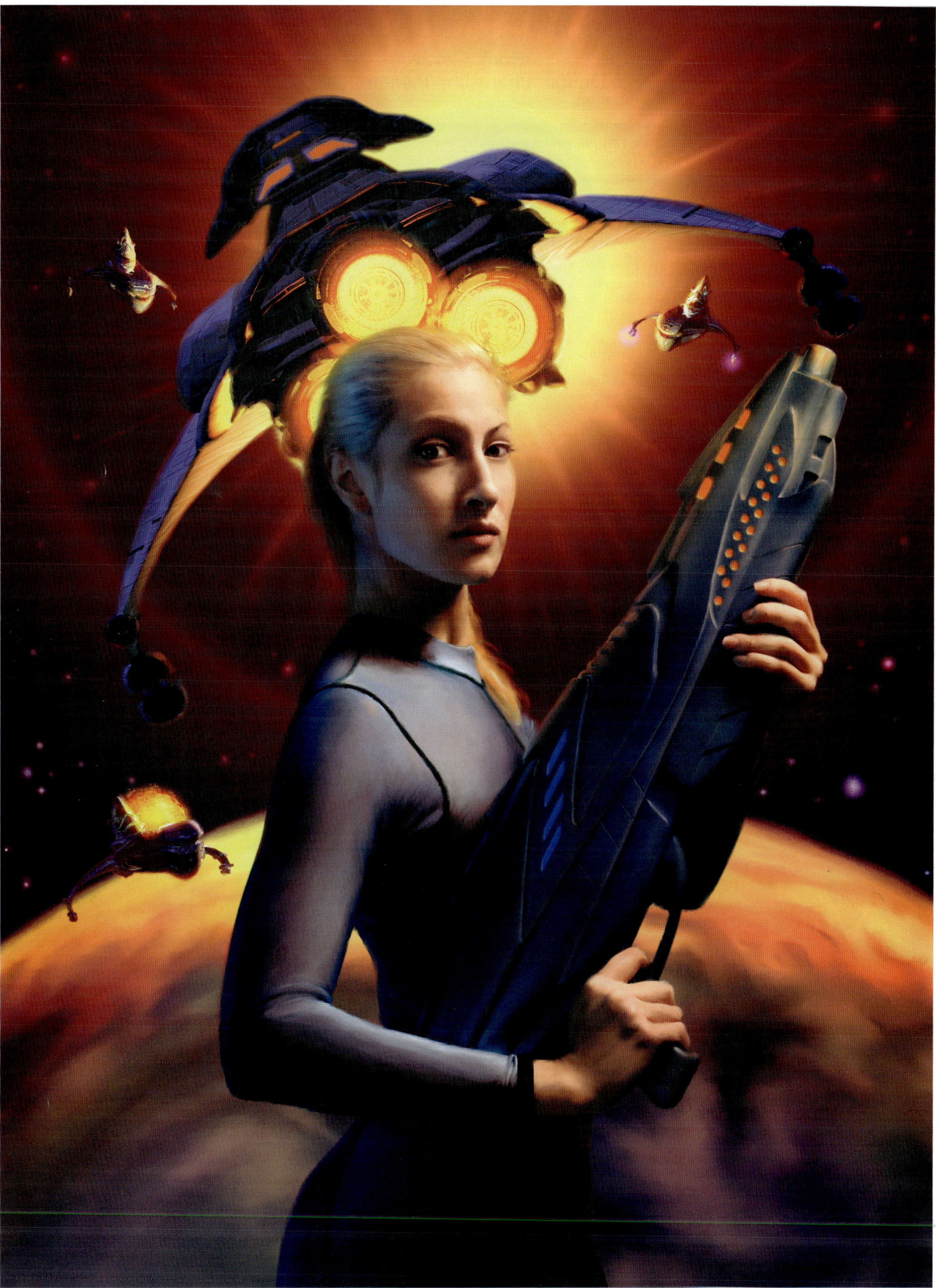

Kris Longknife: Audacious Book 5

Book Cover
Digital: Photoshop/Painter/3D

My favorite of the six, Audacious is a modern interpretation of classic pulp science fiction art. It has an iconic feel to it that evokes nostalgia while maintaining the modern look of the other books in the series.
Here I blended several photographs of Arizona with a 3D planet and then I stylized the colors to get an alien feel. You might also notice a Maxfield Parrish technique in the rocks. He's one of my favorite illustrators and his influence often shows up in my work.

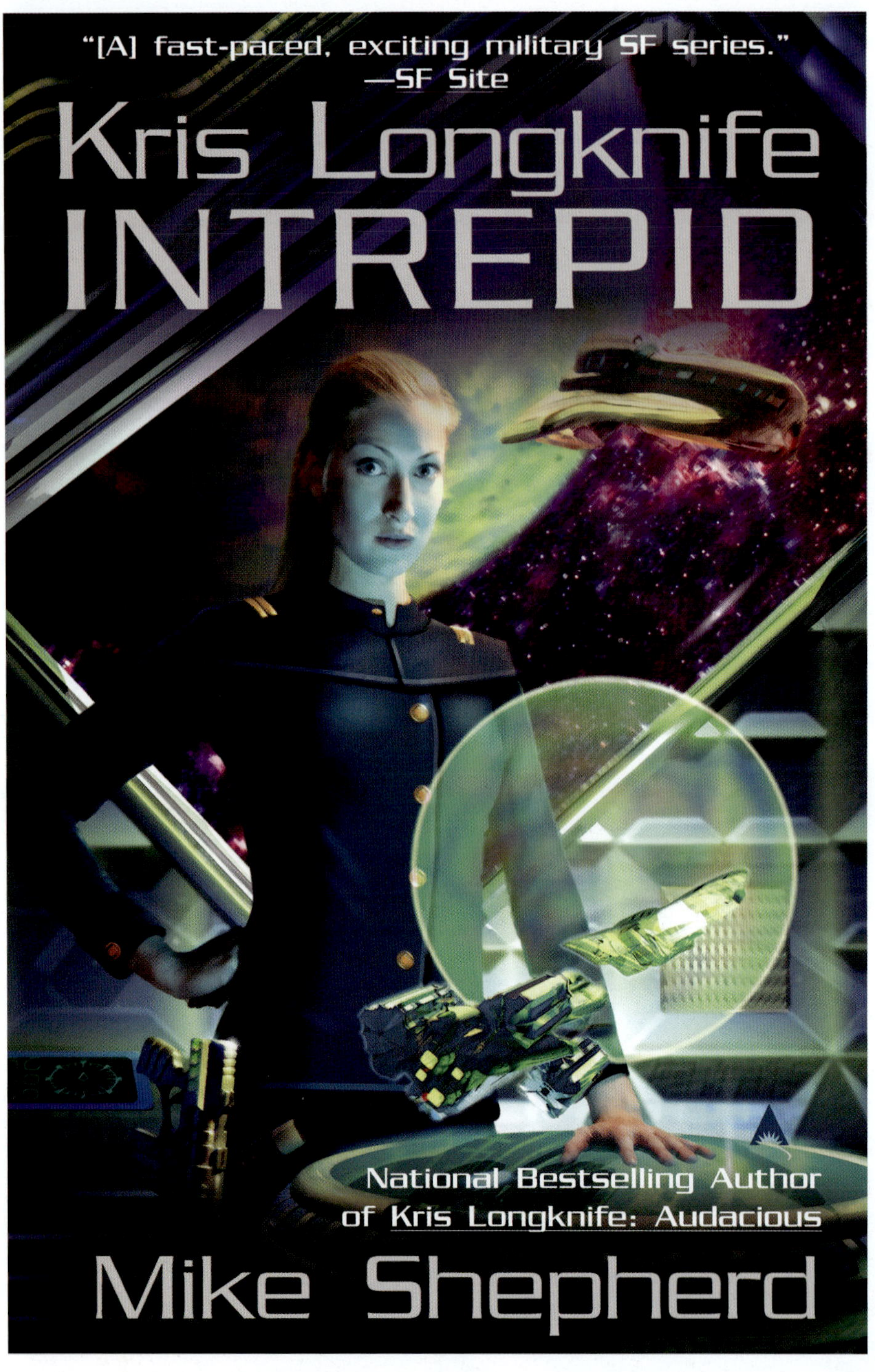

Kris Longknife: Intrepid Book 6

Book Cover
Digital: Photoshop/Painter/3D

A close second favorite to the fifth books art. It has a different feel to it than the other five because it's more of an actual scene. Similar to the fourth book; the portal gives you a peak at the action. In this case I told the story through a hologram depicting the confrontation between the ship in the window and the ship Kris Longknife is commanding.

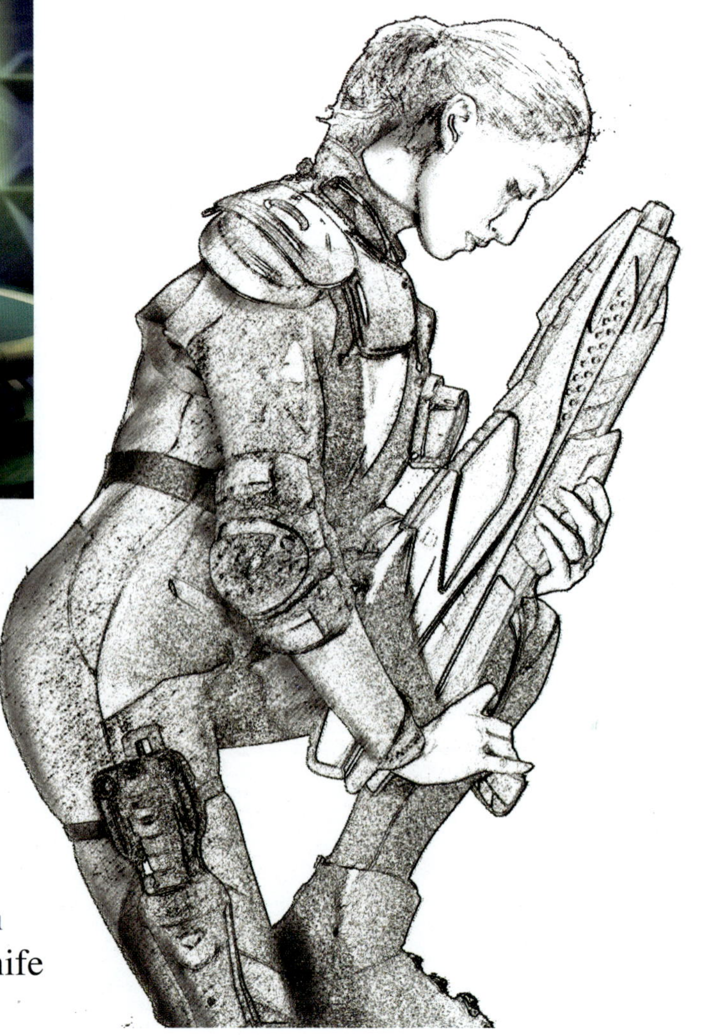

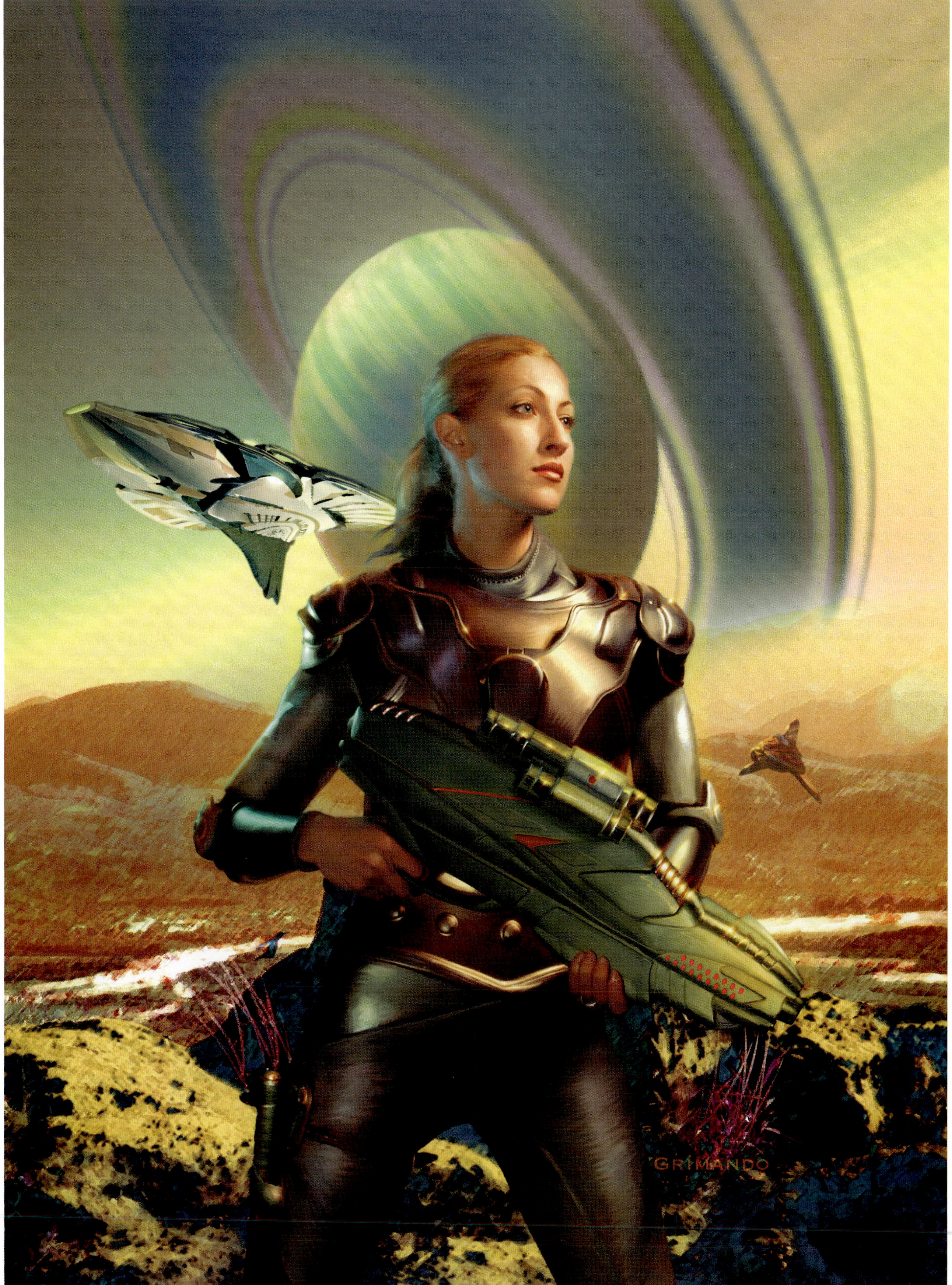
GRIMANDO

Fire Dragon

Realms of Fantasy Cover
Digital: Photoshop/Illustrator/Painter

This is a good example of pushing the illustration into a convincing painting rather then just a composite of photographs. After a rough sketch on paper the initial stage of the illustration is composited in Photoshop (or Painter if you prefer). In Photoshop I'll combine photographic reference (all shot myself) with hand drawn and 3D elements. I can complete the painting in Photoshop but I prefer to bring it to only some level of completion by blending elements edges, blocking in color, adjusting color balance and levels. The finishing stage is a personal preference for the ease of which Painter allows you to use the photos and other elements as an underlying template for which to paint over. It simulates natural brush strokes better than Photoshop (in my opinion). On the other hand if I didn't want the illustration to look like a painting Photoshop is a much better retouching and photo manipulation tool.

The Water Castle

Realms of Fantasy Illustration
Digital: Photoshop/Painter/3D

It can be challenging to balance out a two-page spread or wrap-around cover. You have to leave plenty of room for text and title without compromising the integrity of the piece.

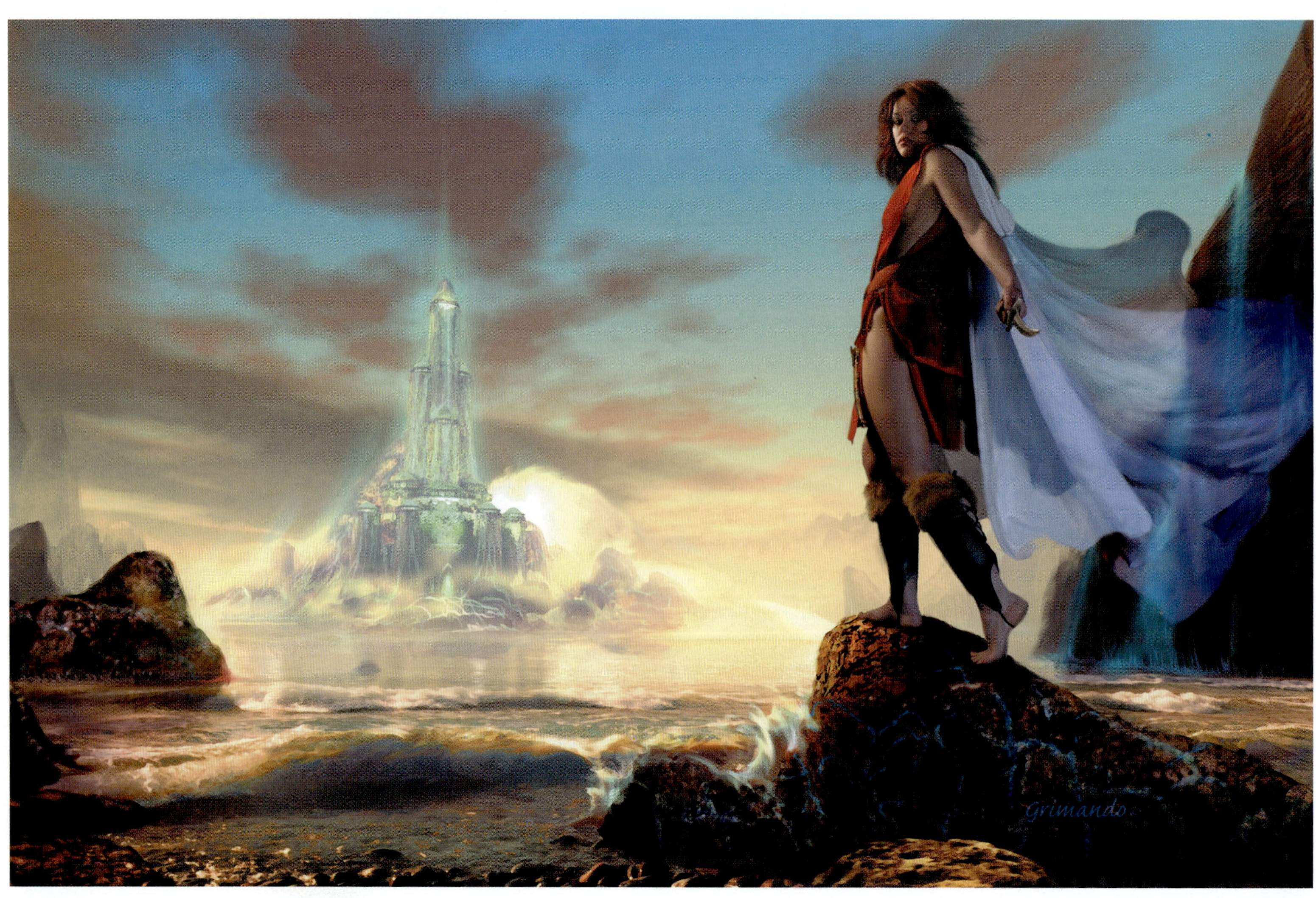

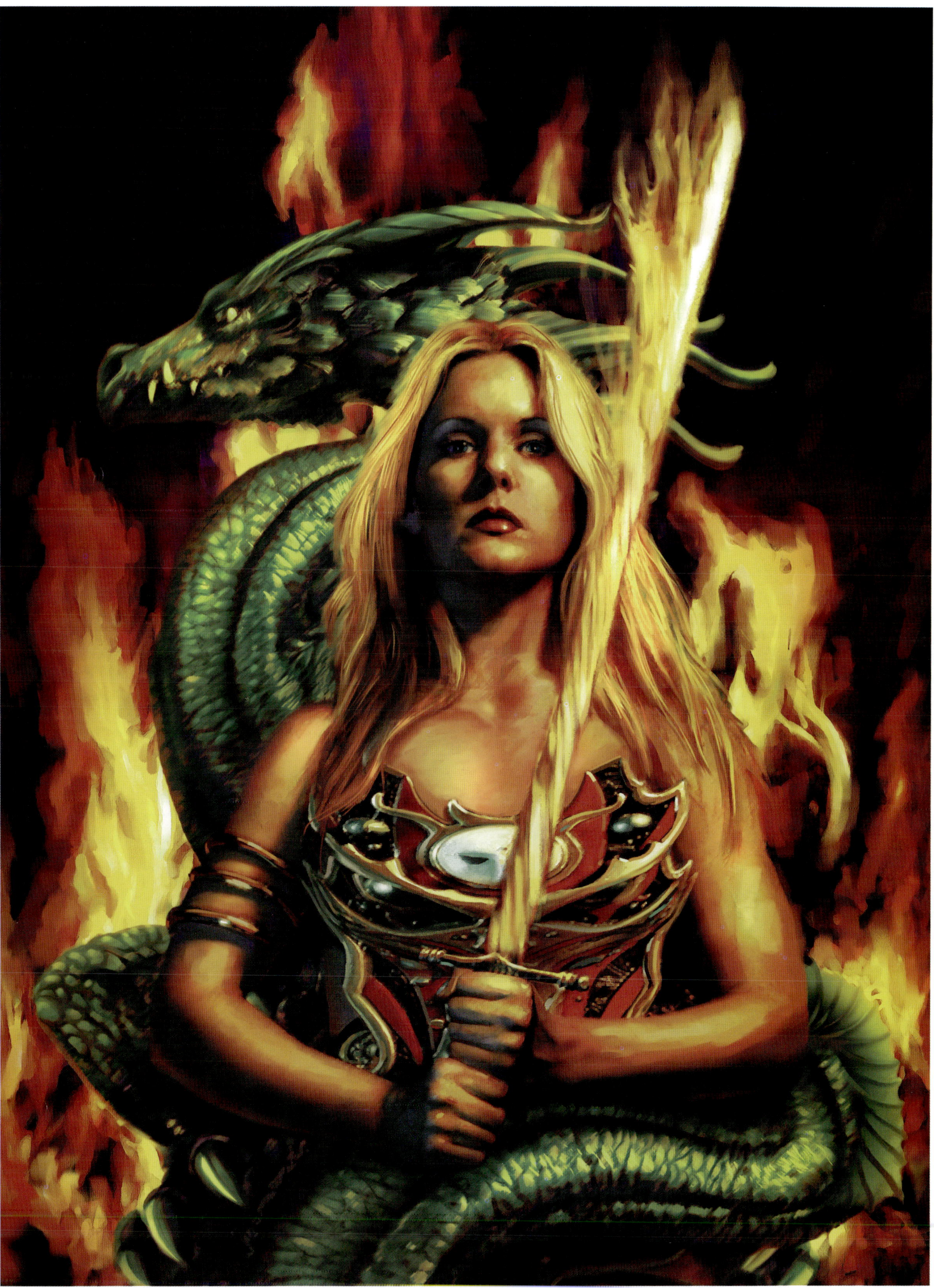

Saturn's Children

Book Cover
Digital: Photoshop/Painter/3D

The art director for the Science Fiction Book Club saw an earlier version of this at a fantasy convention art show. The piece was called, Dream of Flight, and it featured mechanical wings attached to the body suit. He said it would be perfect for a hard cover edition of Saturn's Children. Of course the wings had to come off because it's a story about android sex slaves and they don't fly.

Luckily everything is done in layers with digital illustration. It wasn't exactly easy to remove the wings because they were part of the 3D elements of this piece. I designed the cables protruding from her back in 3D to help the design "travel" from the back cover to the front.

Originally the design started with a combination of a 3D figure and a photographic figure. I matched the pose of the real figure in a program called Poser and added the metal textures. I then added the helmet and wings (or in this case cables).

After matching the lighting I rendering the 3D elements. Bringing them into Photoshop I decided which elements would stay and which would be hidden or how much of her skin would show. I added the background from a tomb I photographed in New Orleans then I stylized it and colored it.

The last phase is to bring the composite into the program Painter and repaint the whole thing. This last stage can take a day or more but it's worth it. The end result is a much more painted or illustrated look.

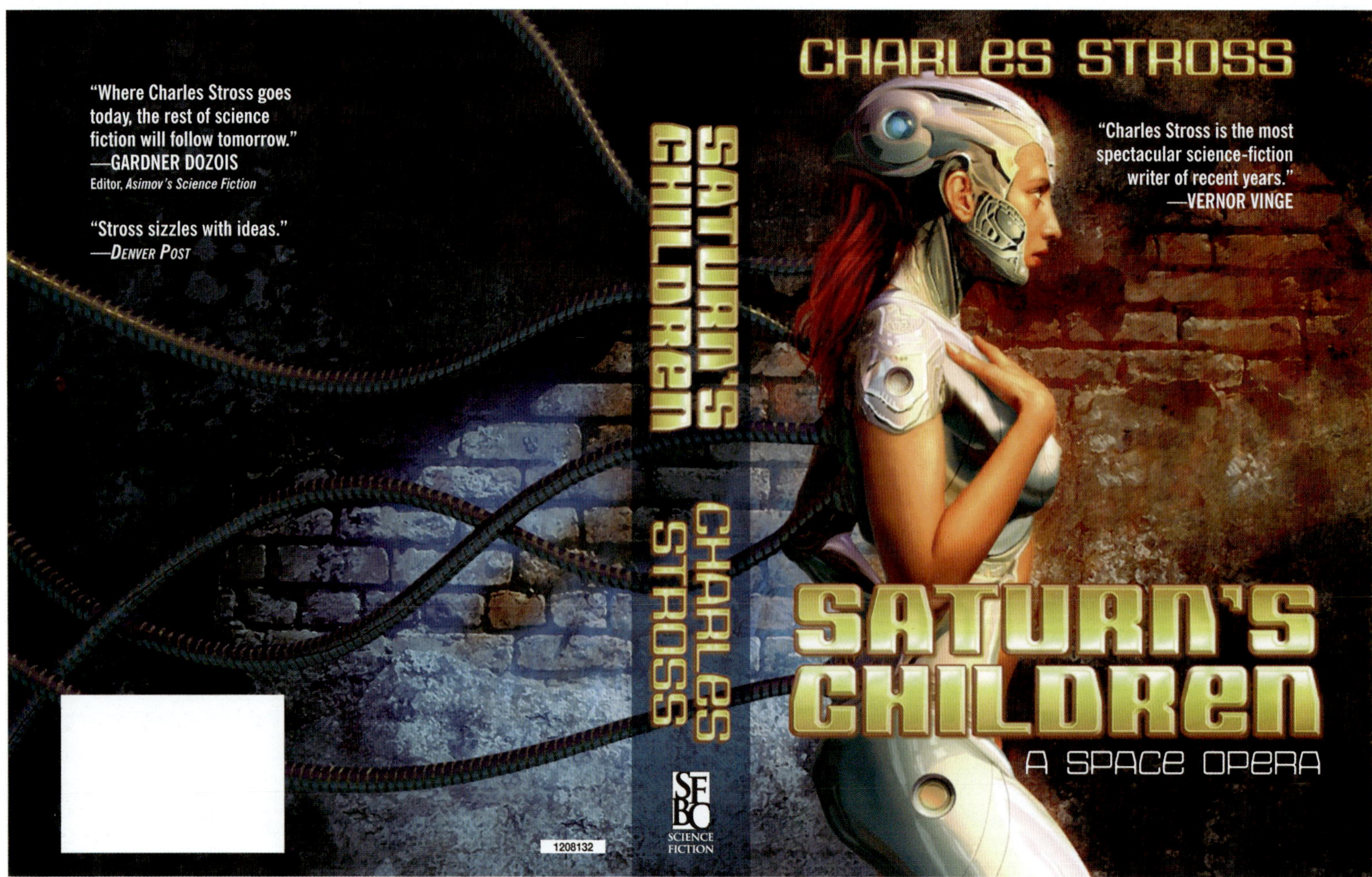

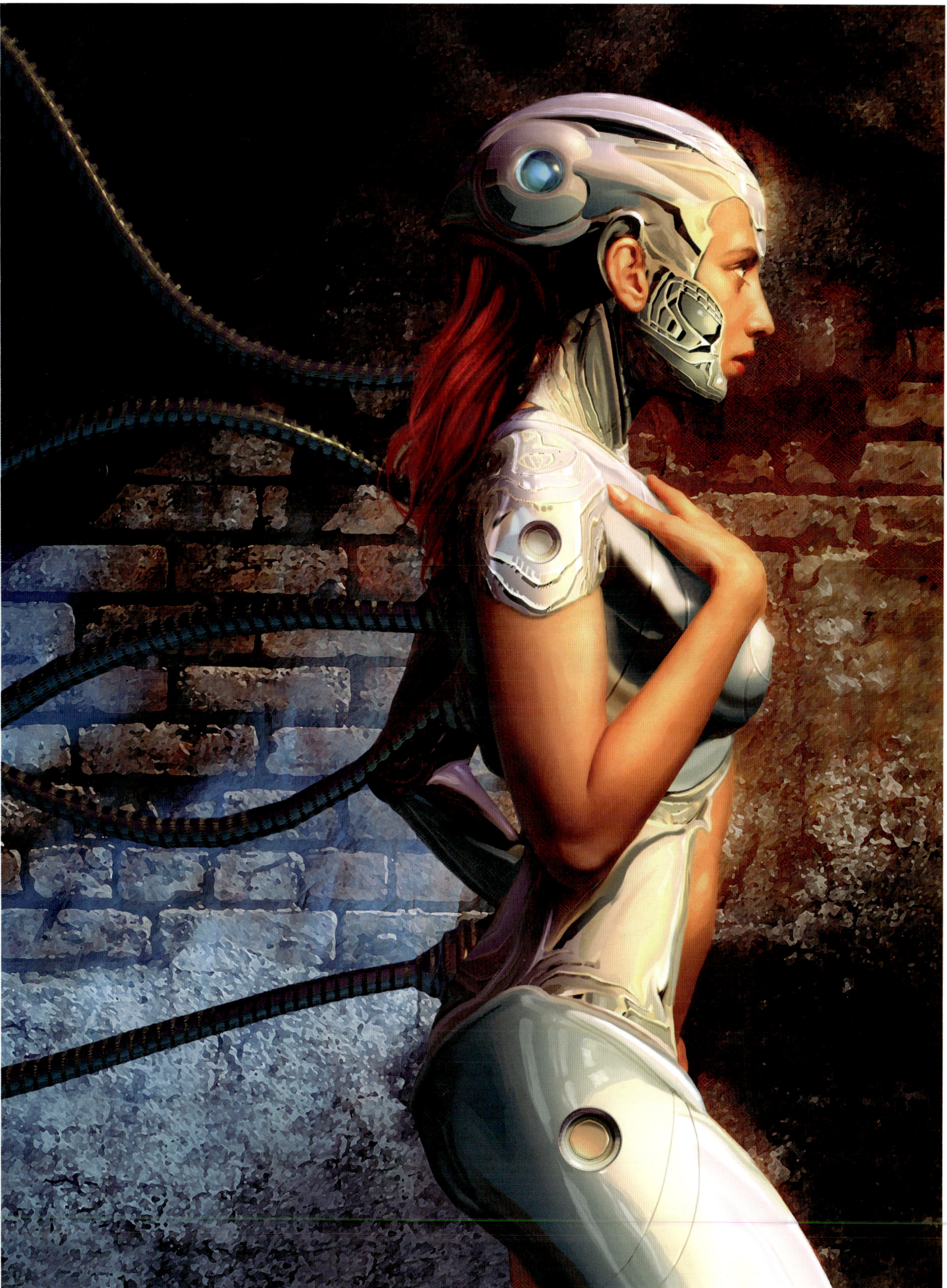

Death, The Devil, and the Lady in White

Realms of Fantasy Illustration
Digital: Photoshop//Painter

This piece was tough from start to finish. Not only for me but the model as well. I tried several times to get a model to look like they're flying with little success. I had them lay on tables and across chairs. I even had them jump up in the air but it never looked natural. Finally it dawned on me that the only way to get a figure to look suspended was to hang them from the ceiling. I screwed a big hook into the beams of my studio ceiling and hung a large strap from it. I then turned on a huge industrial fan for effect. The model was able to do the most amazing things with the strap. She really looked suspended and graceful. This takes a bit of strength so I used a friend from the gym. It takes a good sport to hang from a ceiling for an hour or so. She's since posed for many of my personal pieces. The hard part for me was sketching out ideas for the pose with little-to-no reference before the shoot. I have a copy of a rare out-of-print photography book of woman under water. It came in handy for sketching out the graceful movements of a woman suspended in space.

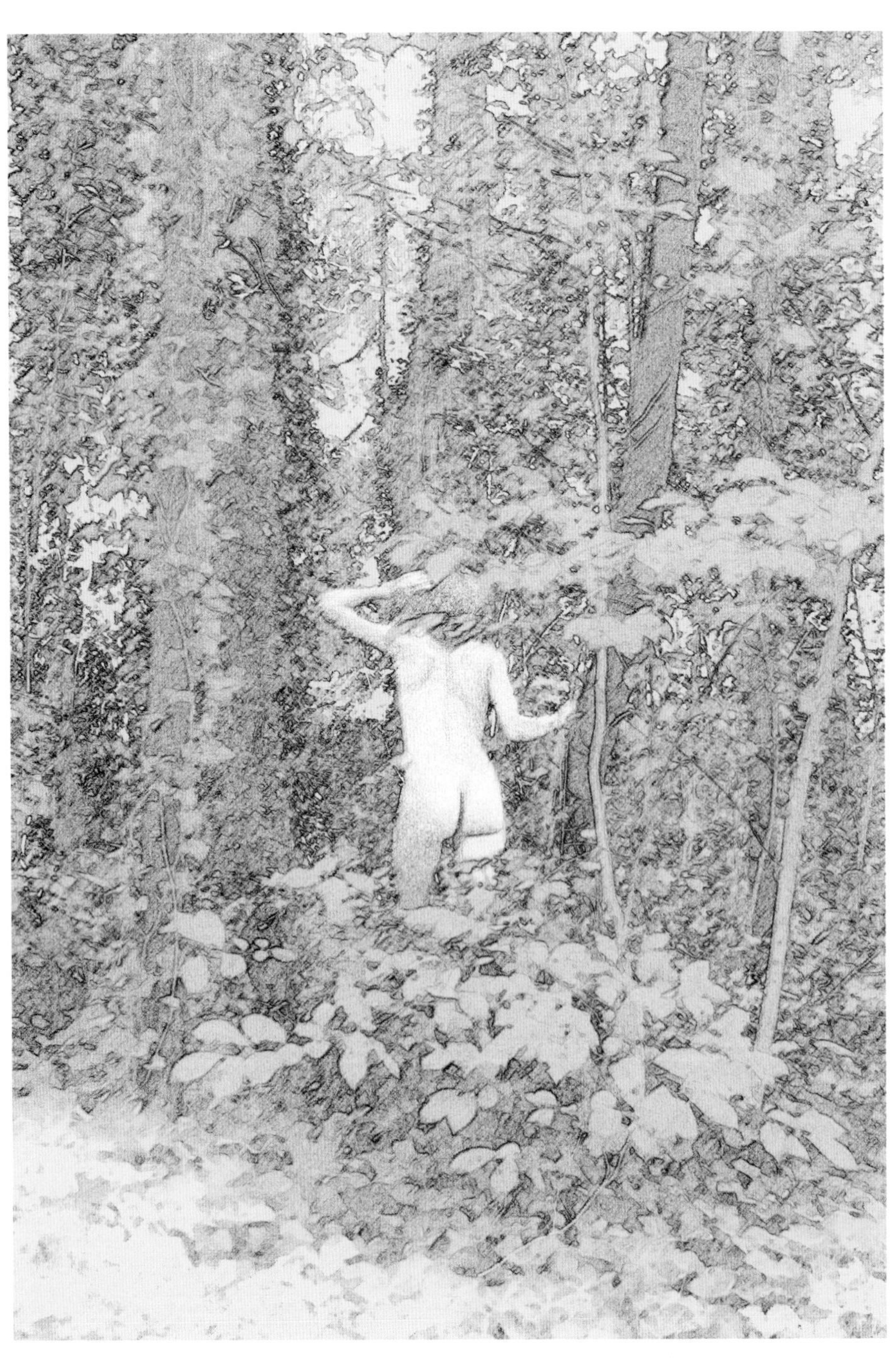

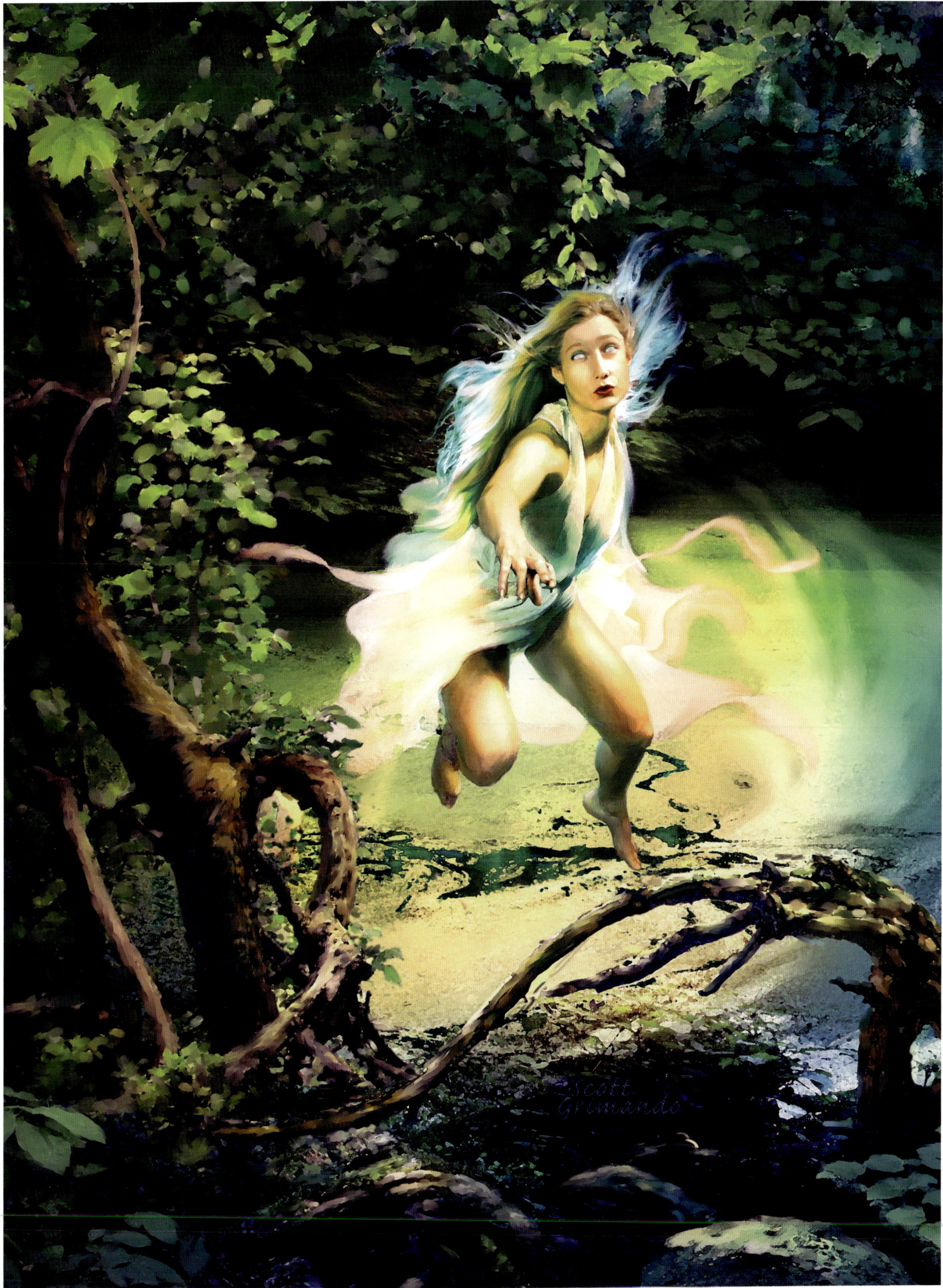
Scott
Grimando

Tribesman of Gor

Book Cover
Digital: Photoshop/Painter/3D

I like to call this my first book cover but really, it's my second. The first one came out so bad that I don't show it anymore. It took me a little while to realize that my job is really more of a designer then a painter. An illustrator is a problem solver. We are presented with a set of criteria for the assignment. There are story elements and the idea that the art director and editors want to get across. An illustrator must take what seems like a very creatively restricting set of guidelines and come up with something that reflects his own unique style. That's the challenge. Coming up with something uniquely you.
You better already know how to paint!

Dark Seed, Dark Stone

Realms of Fantasy Illustration
Digital: Photoshop/Painter/3D

Magazine illustrations never have a budget for a model so you use whoever is around. There's nothing wrong with that as long as you find the right characters. Norman Rockwell did it all the time. He used his friends and family as models and his paintings are that much more believable for it.
In this case I used myself as the barbarian king and my landlord's daughter for the princess. I think we both suited the roles well.

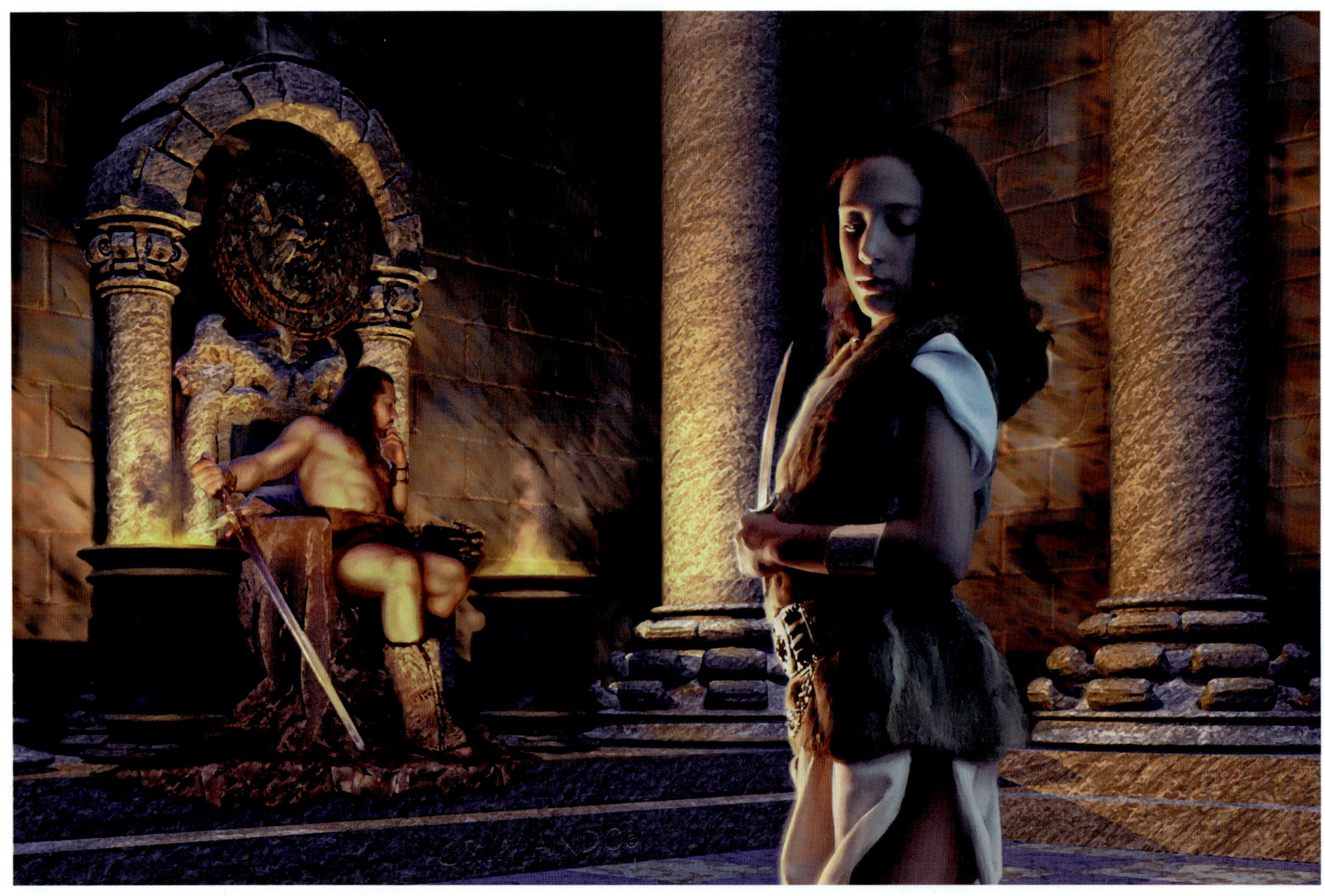

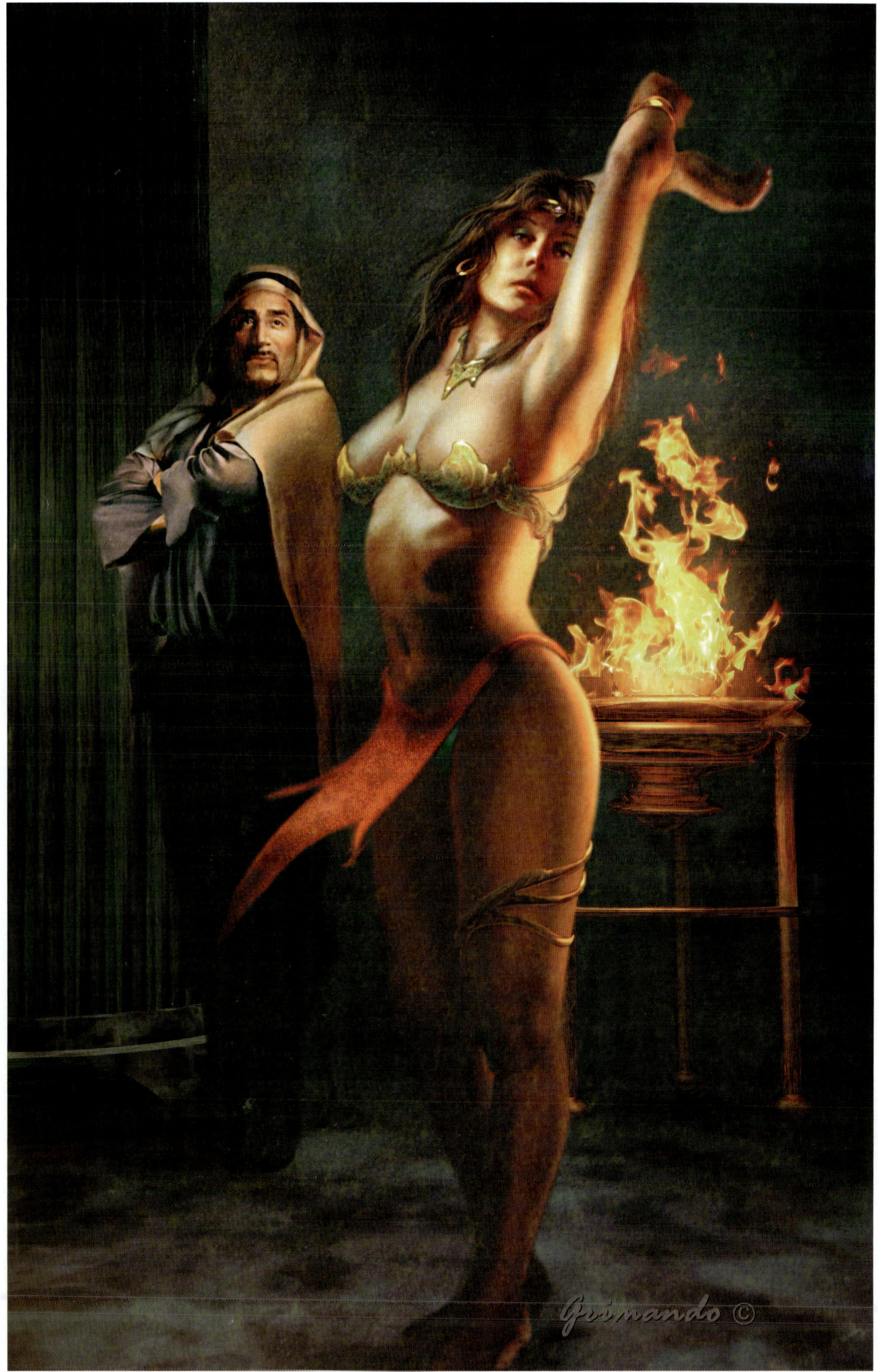
Gismando ©

The Aware: Isle of Glory Book 1

Book Cover

Digital: Photoshop/Painter/3D

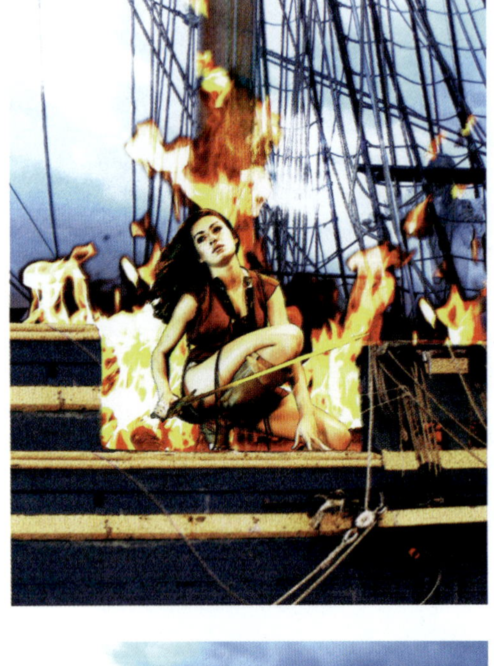

To the right is the first of three U.S. editions of the popular Australian series.

To the left are three roughs for, The Tainted, the third book in the series. The protagonist from the first book makes a return so I was able to use the first model again. Luckily she was available. The model is my step-niece.

The series of roughs shows the whittling down process that an illustrator goes through working with an art director.

The first rough had a pose the A.D. liked and the second had the ship in the distance she preferred. At some point she decided a dock would be better than the beach to set the figure in foreground.

The final art for, The Tainted, is featured below.

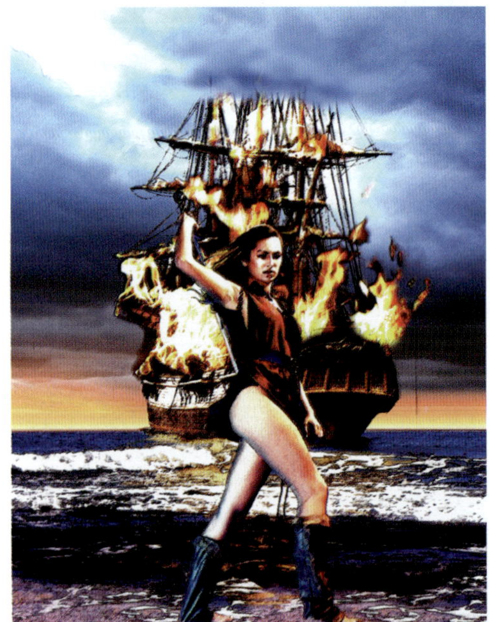

The creature for the Aware and the Tainted was created by combining photographs of a weird-looking but pretty fish called a Sea Robin. Most fishermen consider it a nuisance but I've always loved its fins and the hard dragon-like skull.

It also croaks so what's not to love?

Keep in mind that a huge amount of manipulation is done to the photos to get the creature to not look like a fish.

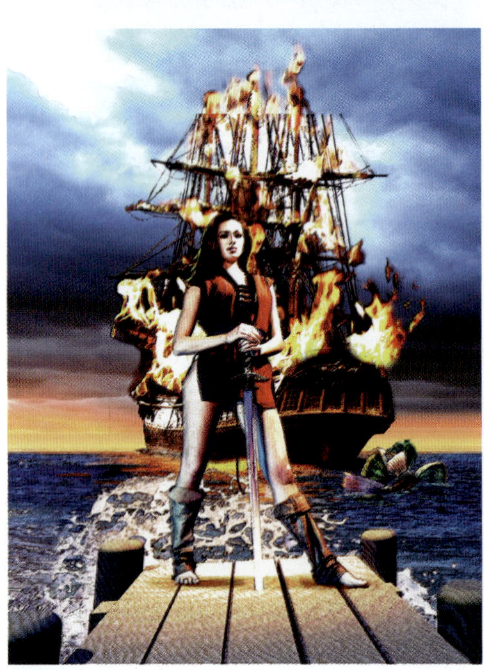

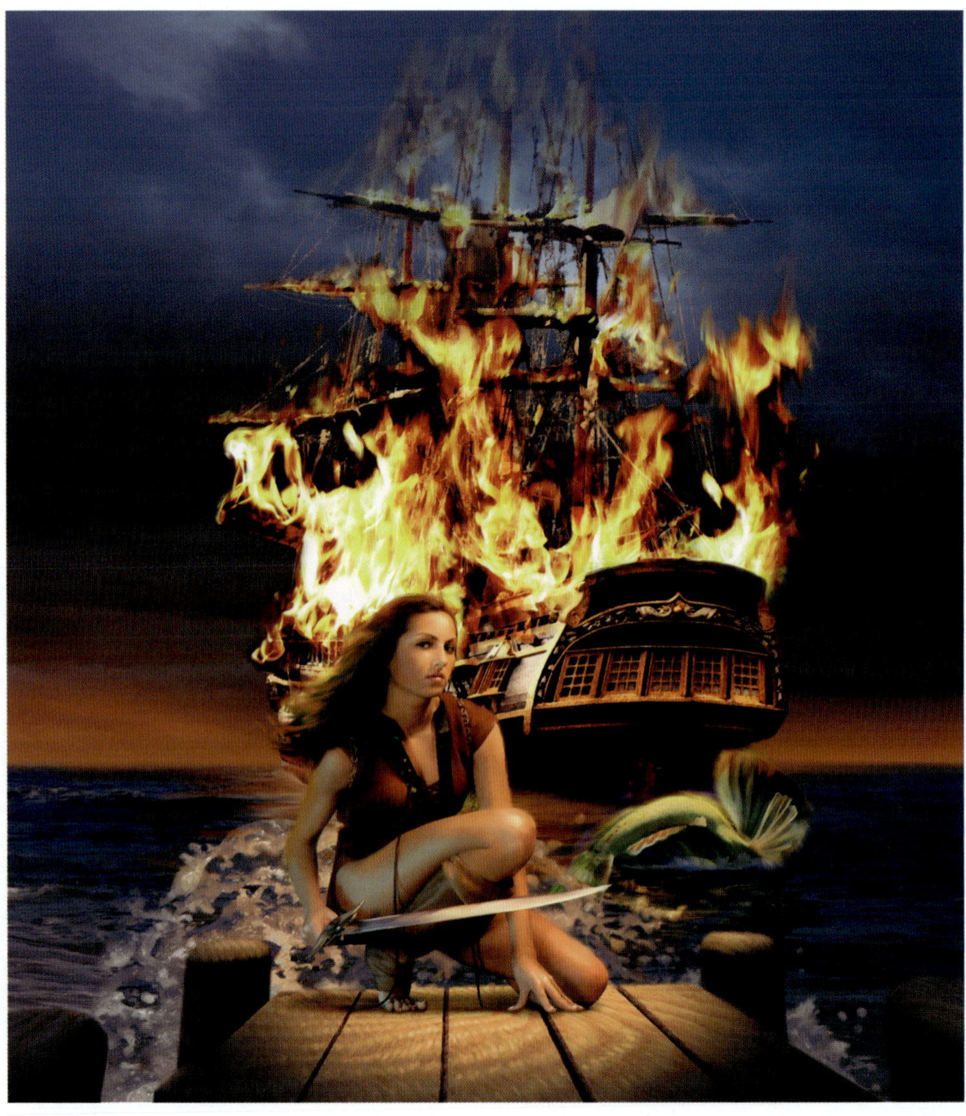

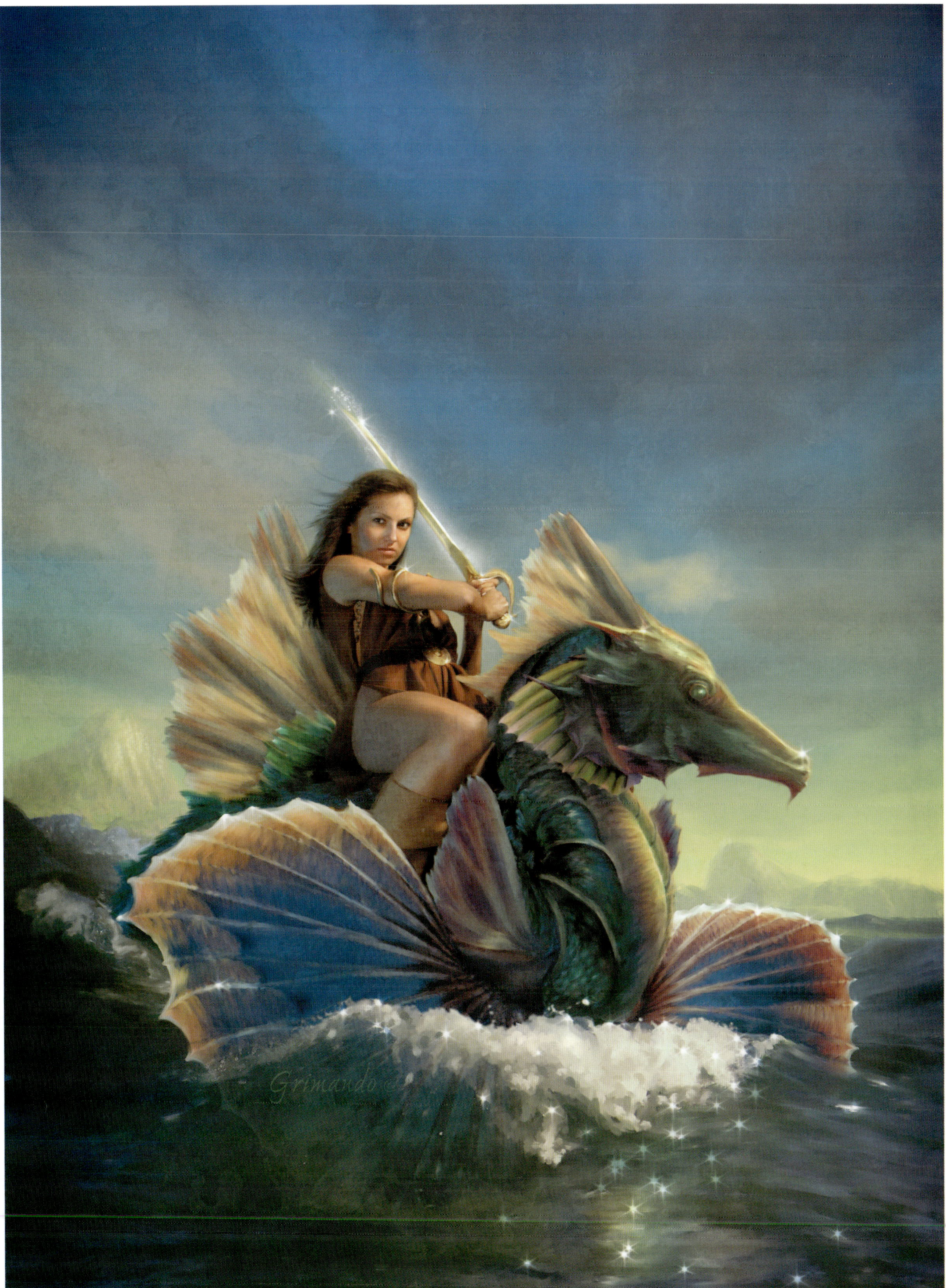
Grimando

Gilfeather: Isle of Glory Book 2

Book Cover
Digital: Photoshop/Painter/3D

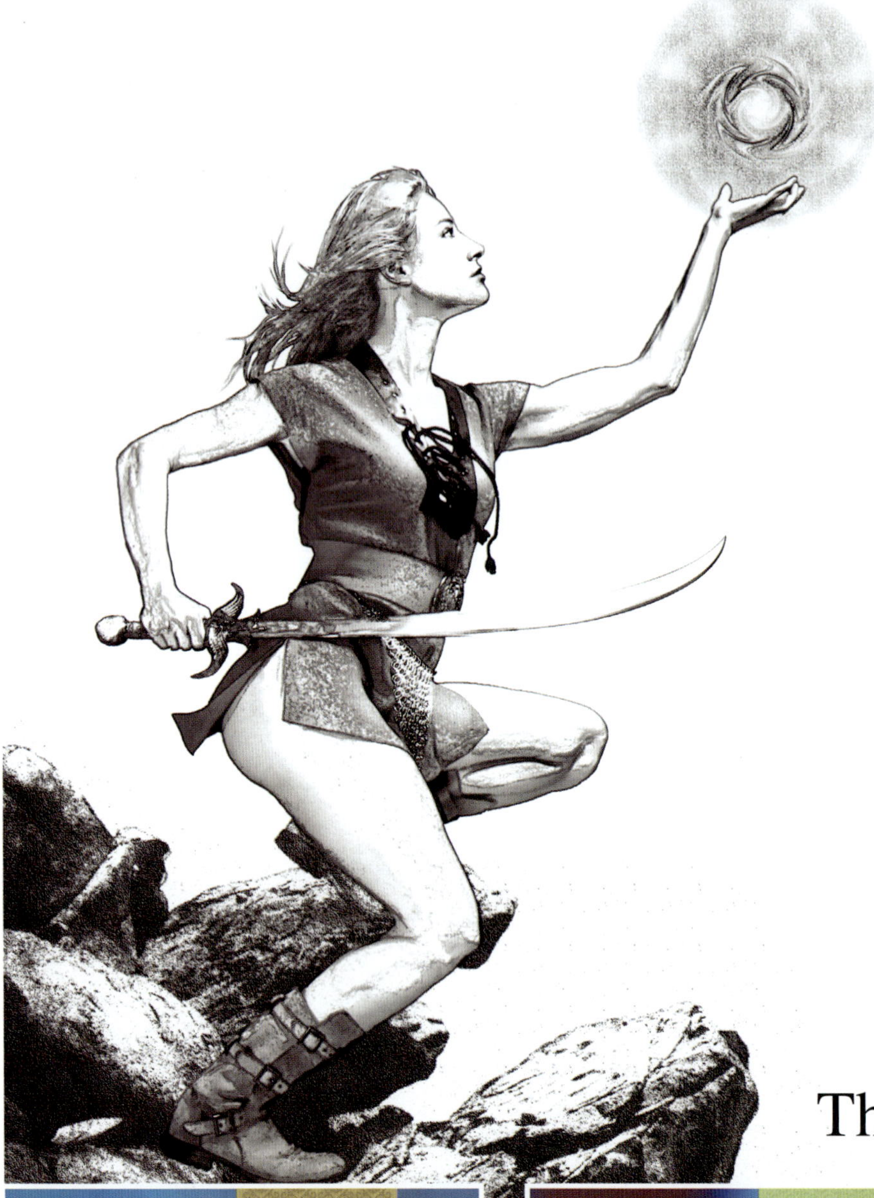

In the second book of the Isle of Glory series a new character takes the lead roll. To find a new face I used a local modeling agency. They're often more than happy to send you head shots you can show to the art director because a local agency needs to show its models that they're doing something. Even if it's a low fee book cover-modeling job it gives the model a tear sheet they can use for their portfolio.

I lucked out with this one. This model was great and I've done lots of portfolio work with her since.

The Isles of Glory Trilogy

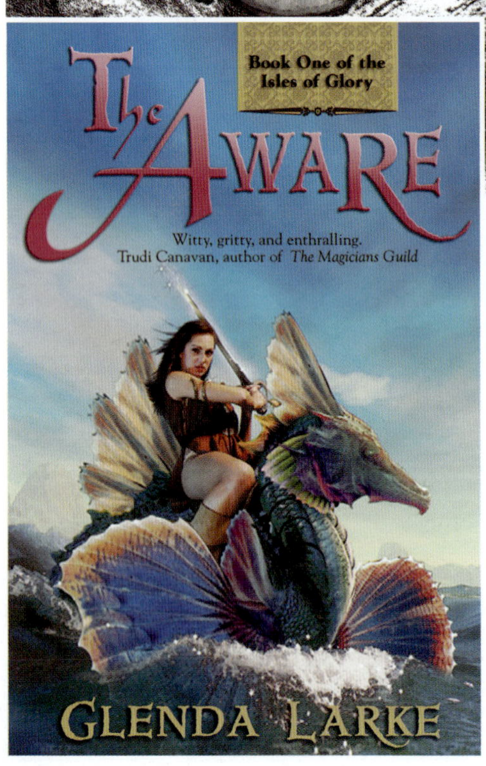

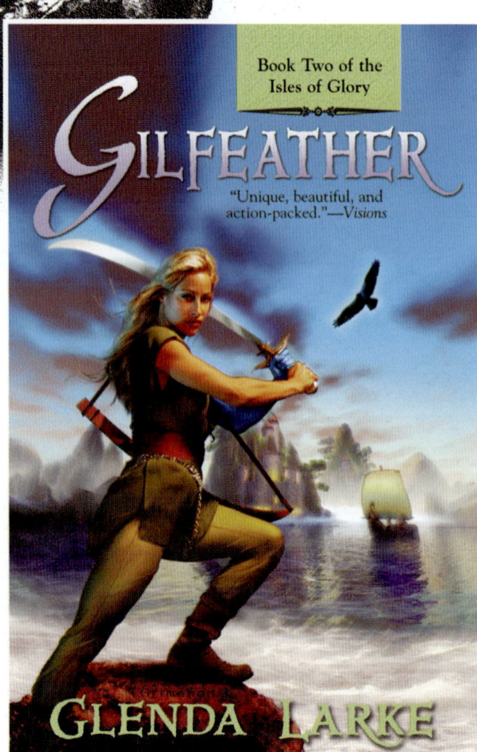

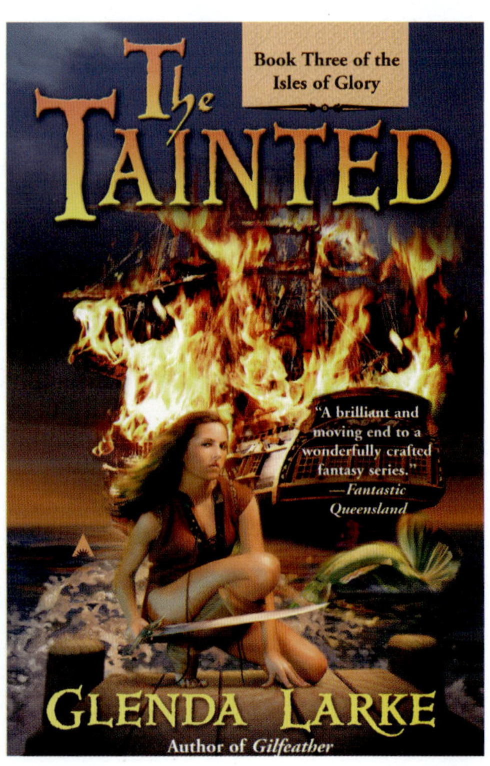

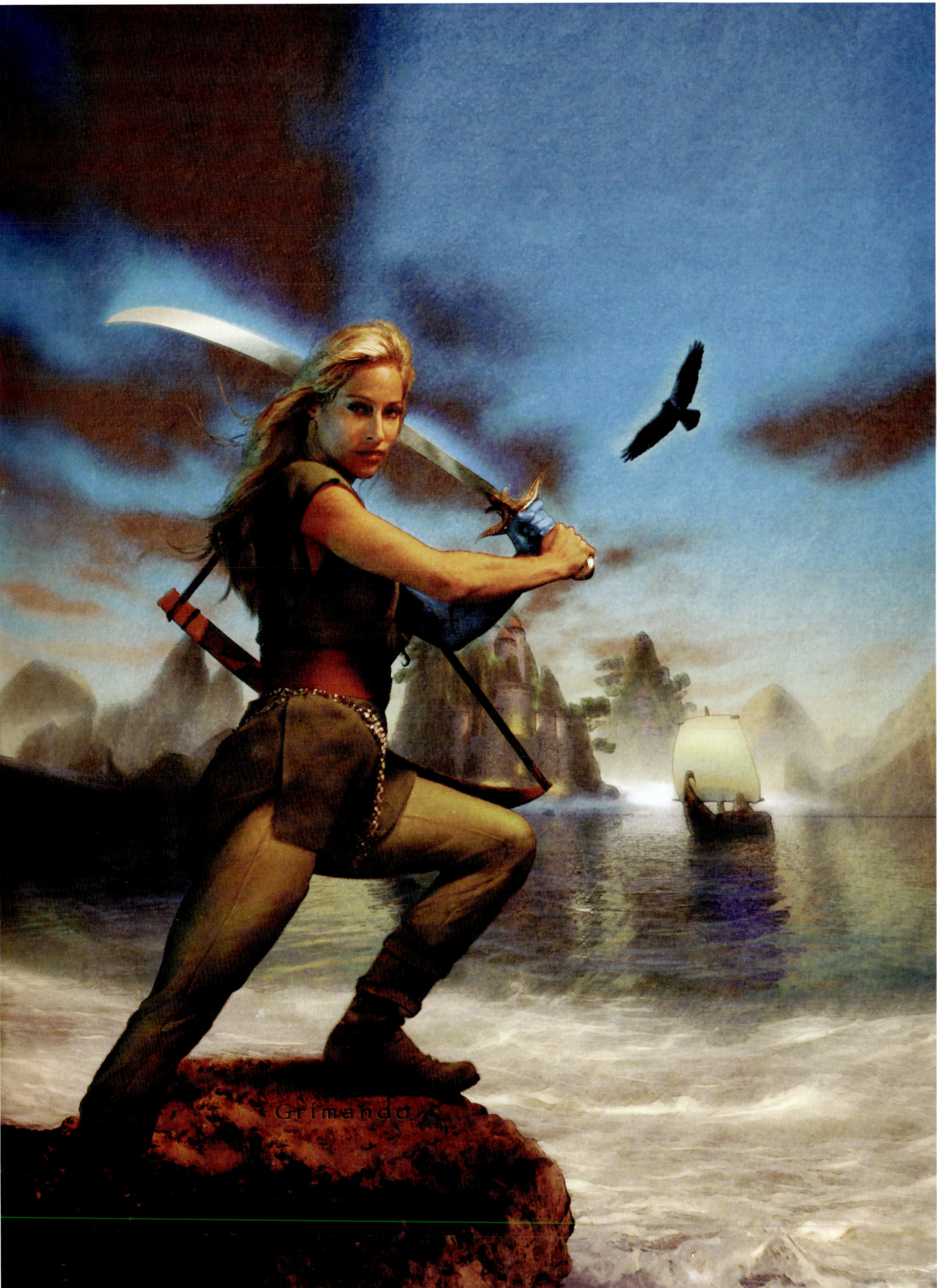
Grimando ©

Witch World

Book Cover
Digital: Photoshop/Painter

My photography assistant and I originally posed for the rough comp of this cover. I'm too stocky for most cover characters. I make a better troll, ogre, alien or barbarian king. In the first stage of a cover the artist needs to produce rough sketches and/or color roughs to show to the art directors. I use whomever's around for that part. After approval of the rough I called some of my favorite models for this one. My friend Pete is always on call when I need him. He's an artist too, so he enjoys the process.

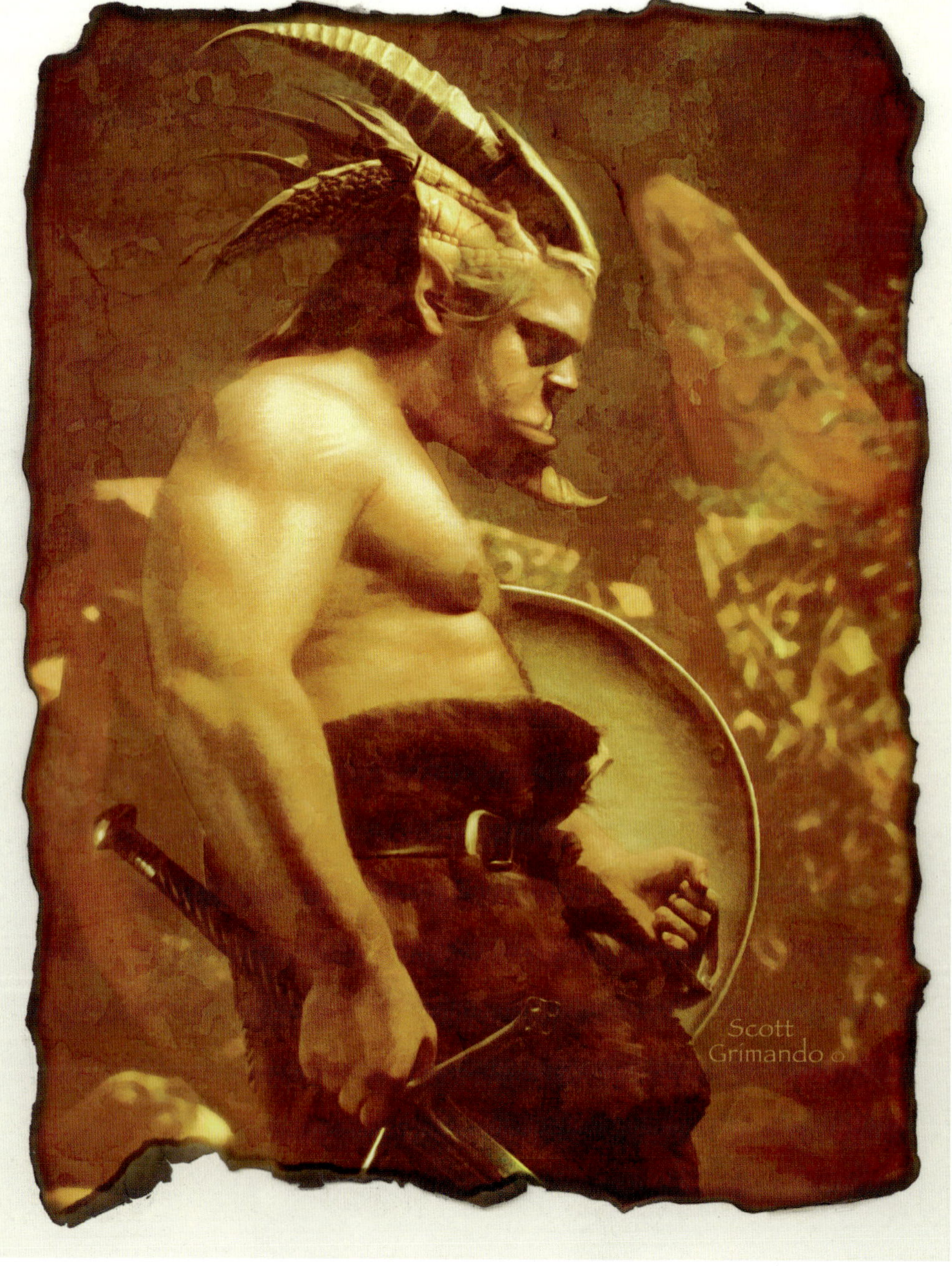

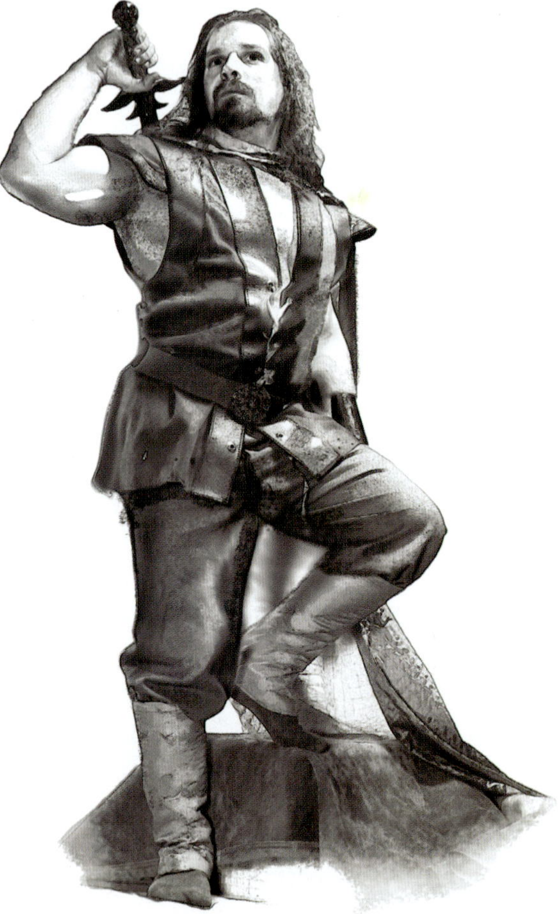

Ogre

Self Portrait
Photoshop/Painter/Mixed Media

This is my favorite self-portrait. I shoot this kind of reference myself using the timer on the camera so that I don't feel self-conscious about getting into character.

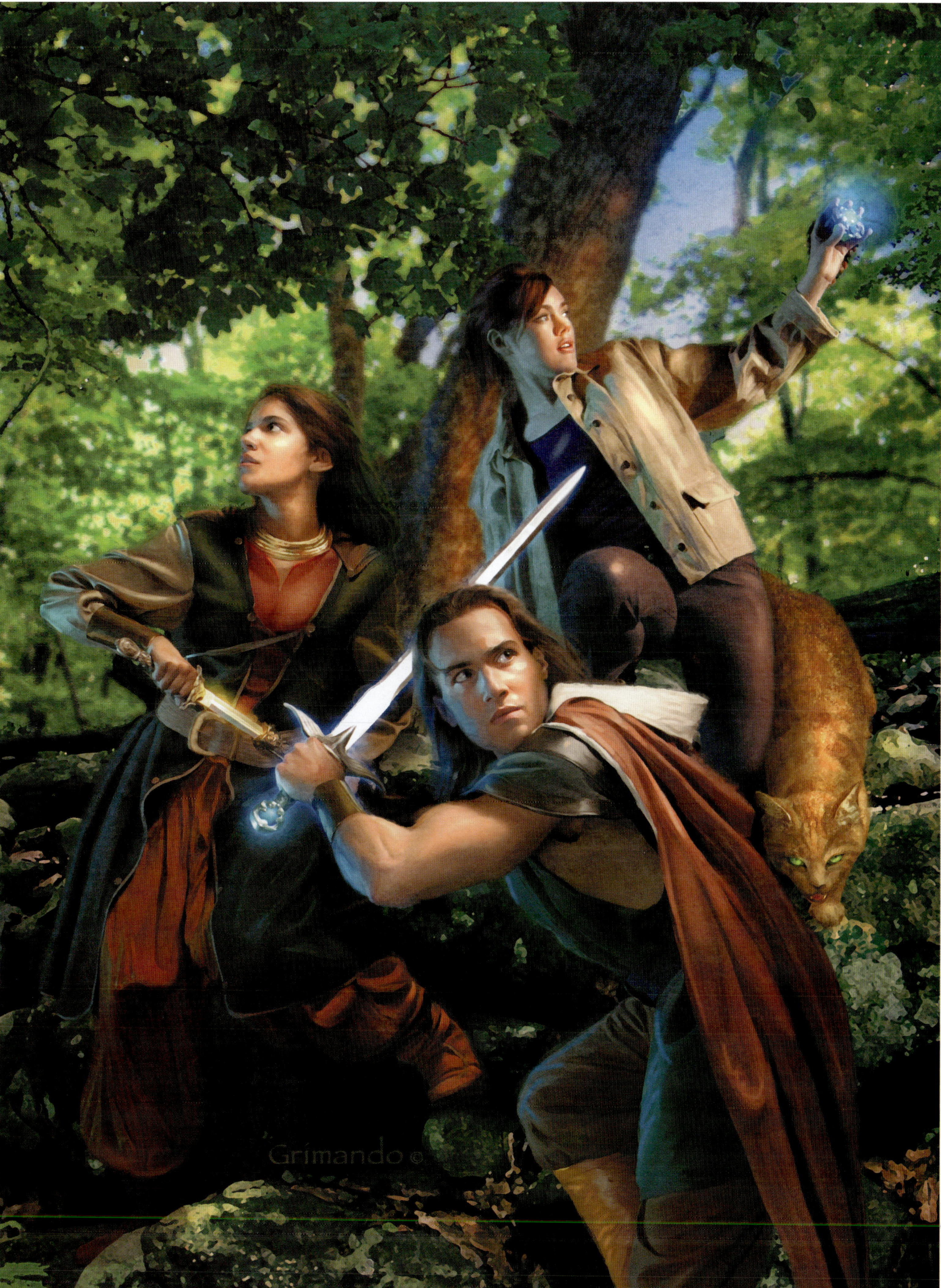
Grimando ©

Beyond The Sun

Book Cover/Poster/Greeting Card
Digital: Photoshop/Painter/3D

This piece was originally designed for the legendary guitarist Ritchie Blackmore and his Blackmore's Night CD cover. It was an overly ambitious project that the record company envisioned. They wanted me to do an illustration for every song. Communication problems with the German record company made completing the project impossible but I negotiated an advance which covered most of the work I did and allowed me to maintain full rights to the cover image.

Since then I've sold the art as a poster, greeting card and a book cover.

I used my friend Pete again in this illustration as a stand-in for Ritchie Blackmore. The models were supposed to be generic enough that they could be mistaken for Ritchie and his wife Candice Night.

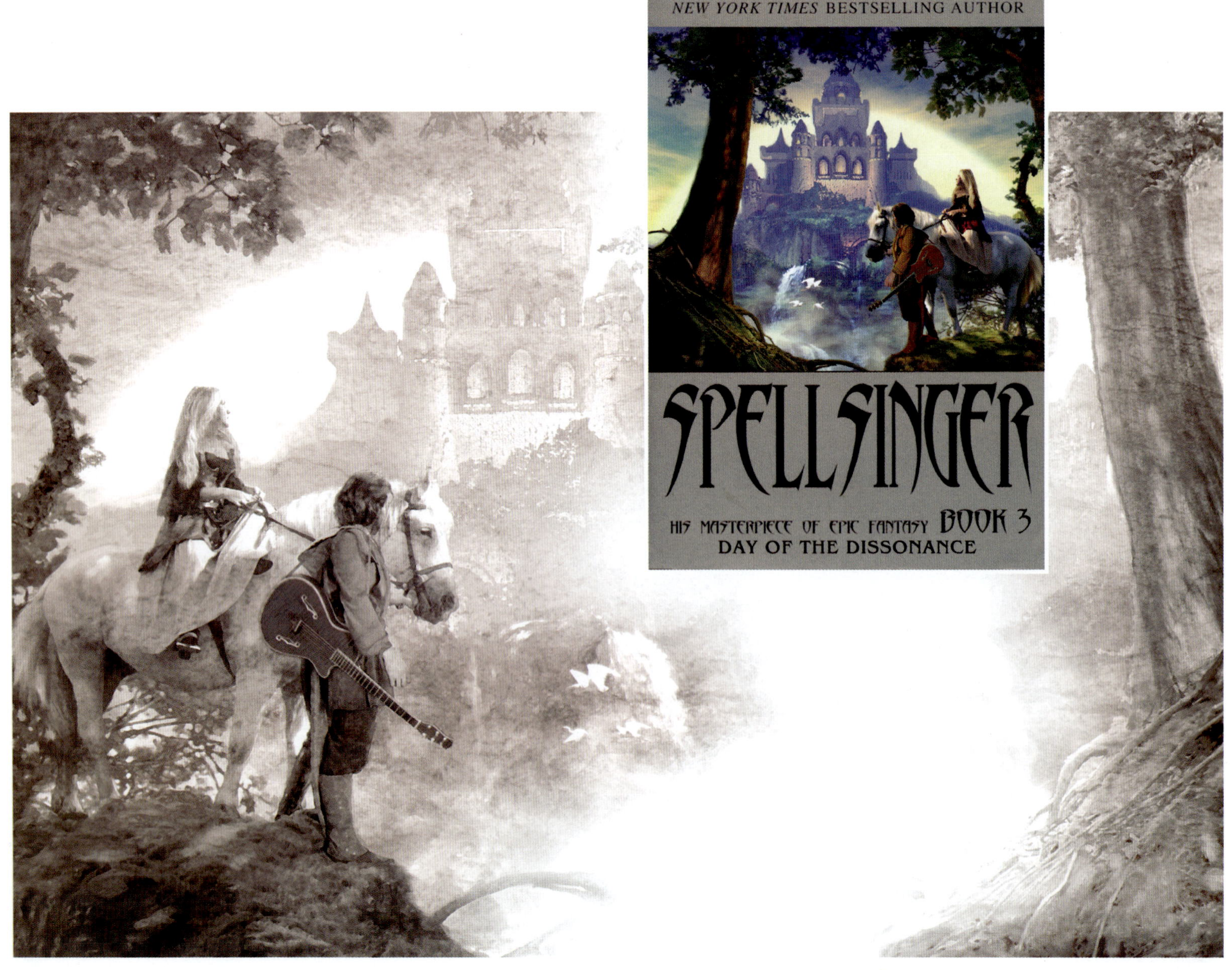

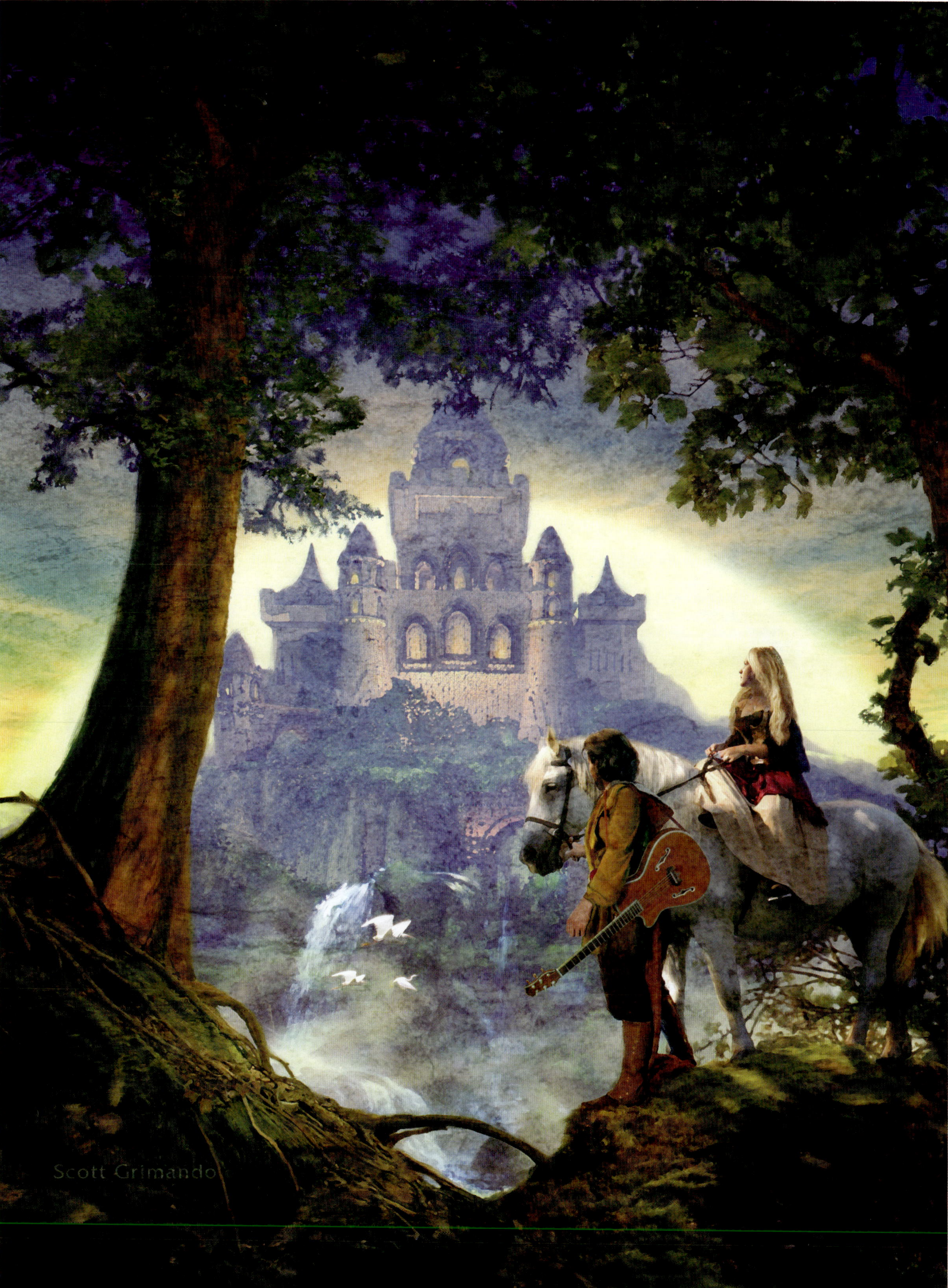
Scott Grimando

Nightwings

Realms of Fantasy/iBooks
Oils on Masonite
18" x 24"

This piece was originally designed for a Realms story by Alan Dean Foster called Wait-A-While. I included a sketched version with wings on the back of a promotional postcard that I sent to publishers. iBooks thought it was perfect for the Silverberg classic Nightwings. Robert Silverberg is one of my favorite science fiction authors so I was very excited about the cover.

A short time later I had the pleasure of meeting Silverberg and his wife at a publishers party. I was very nervous about introducing myself, which is not at all like me. I just didn't want to seem like a weird fan.

I got my nerve up and told him that I was the artist responsible for the new Nightwings cover. He seemed excited and asked his wife if that was the one they made into a cake for him recently. His wife responded warmly, "No that was a different one".

And that was the end of that. My ego was too crushed to gather myself up and try to discuss my favorite books with him.

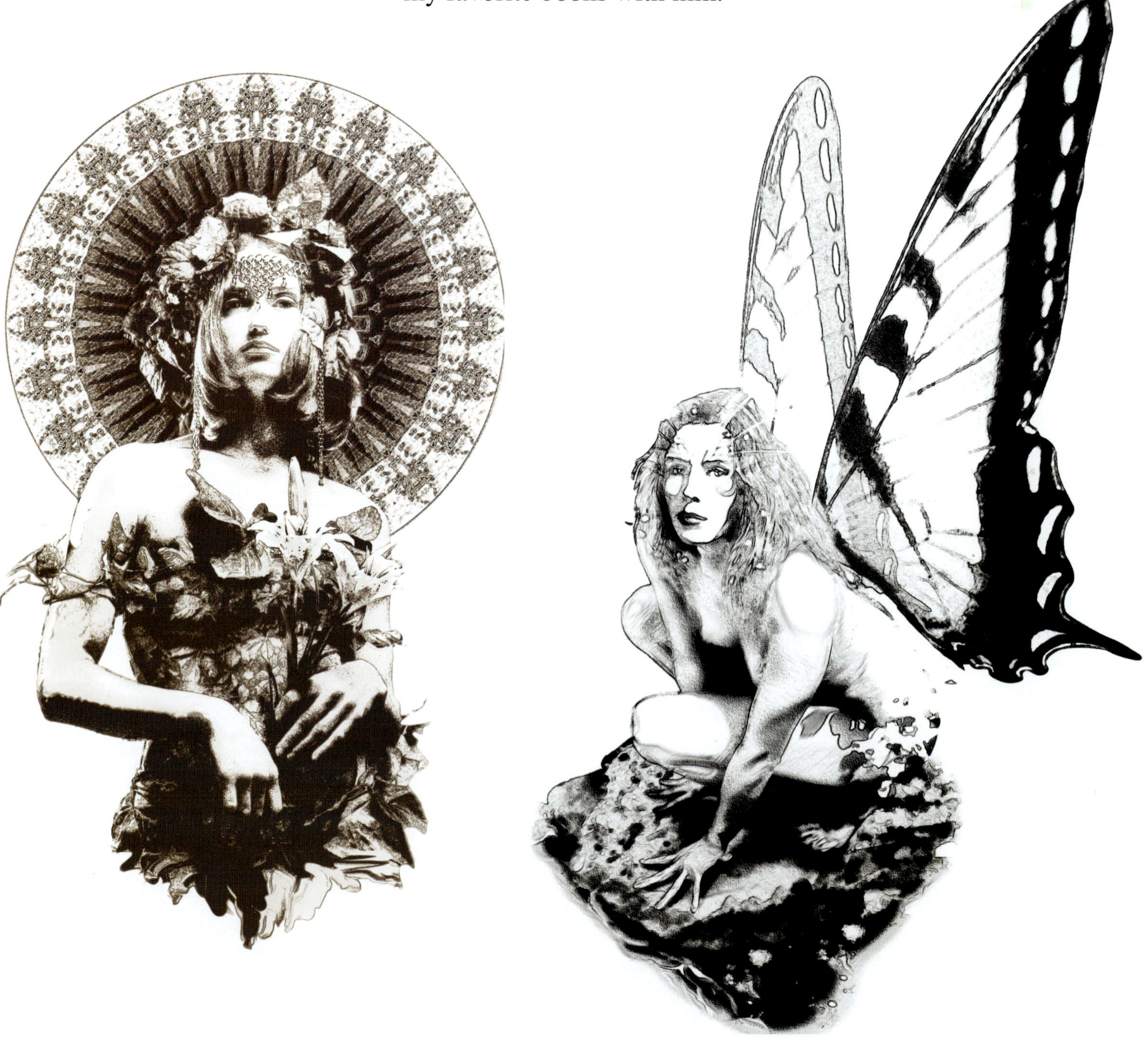

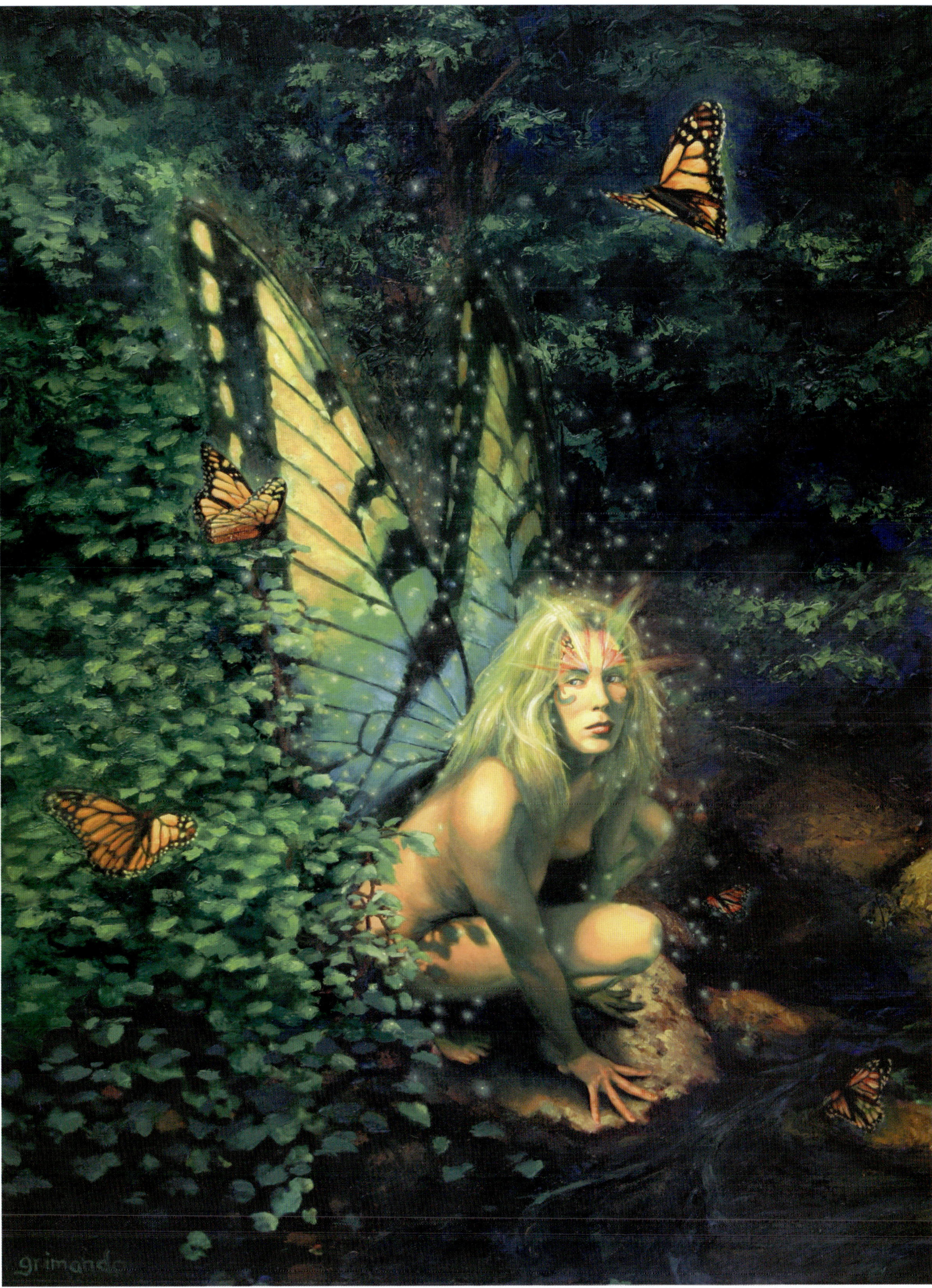

Personal Work

As a child I had a vision. I dreamed of 3-dimensional painting. I don't mean to date myself but when I was young no one had a personal computer and no one thought they ever would. The vision took the form of a cardboard box that I could place clouds in and paint with light. I saw it as going beyond the canvas and I somehow knew that one day I would.

Today I like to call it Etherealization, to go beyond the canvas. I use the computer for all of my commercial work because of the flexibility of the tool. It's important to be able to respond to the clients needs quickly in this fast paced industry.

I use the computer as a tool in my personal work as well because of it's flexibility. I can explore color, light and composition in ways I never could have before the digital age. My skills as a painter go hand in hand with my computer skills. Even the fine art world is now beginning to accept this new medium as a valid art form.

Has art ever really been about the medium used or instead about the vision of the artist using it? You can give a monkey a computer but all he's going to do is spell out "banana".

My personal work runs the gamut from strictly digital art to purely traditional oil paintings. I'm trying to express my own design aesthetic: my own unique vision in what ever form that takes.

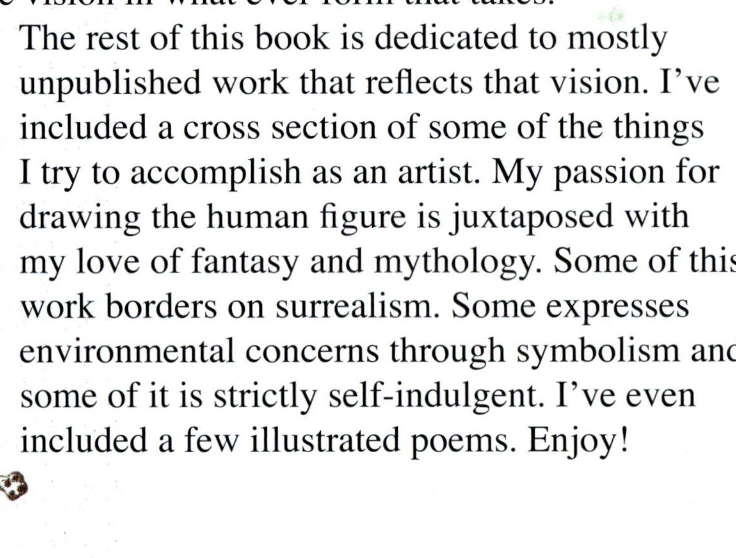

The rest of this book is dedicated to mostly unpublished work that reflects that vision. I've included a cross section of some of the things I try to accomplish as an artist. My passion for drawing the human figure is juxtaposed with my love of fantasy and mythology. Some of this work borders on surrealism. Some expresses environmental concerns through symbolism and some of it is strictly self-indulgent. I've even included a few illustrated poems. Enjoy!

Wood Nymph

Photoshop/Painter

One of the things I've been trying to do with my personal work is to capture the inner light of the subject. I want the figure to be both a part of its environment and the light that illuminates it. Note the warm against cool color patterns that help the subject jump out. Everything I don't want to stand out is softer, less detailed and more monochromatic.

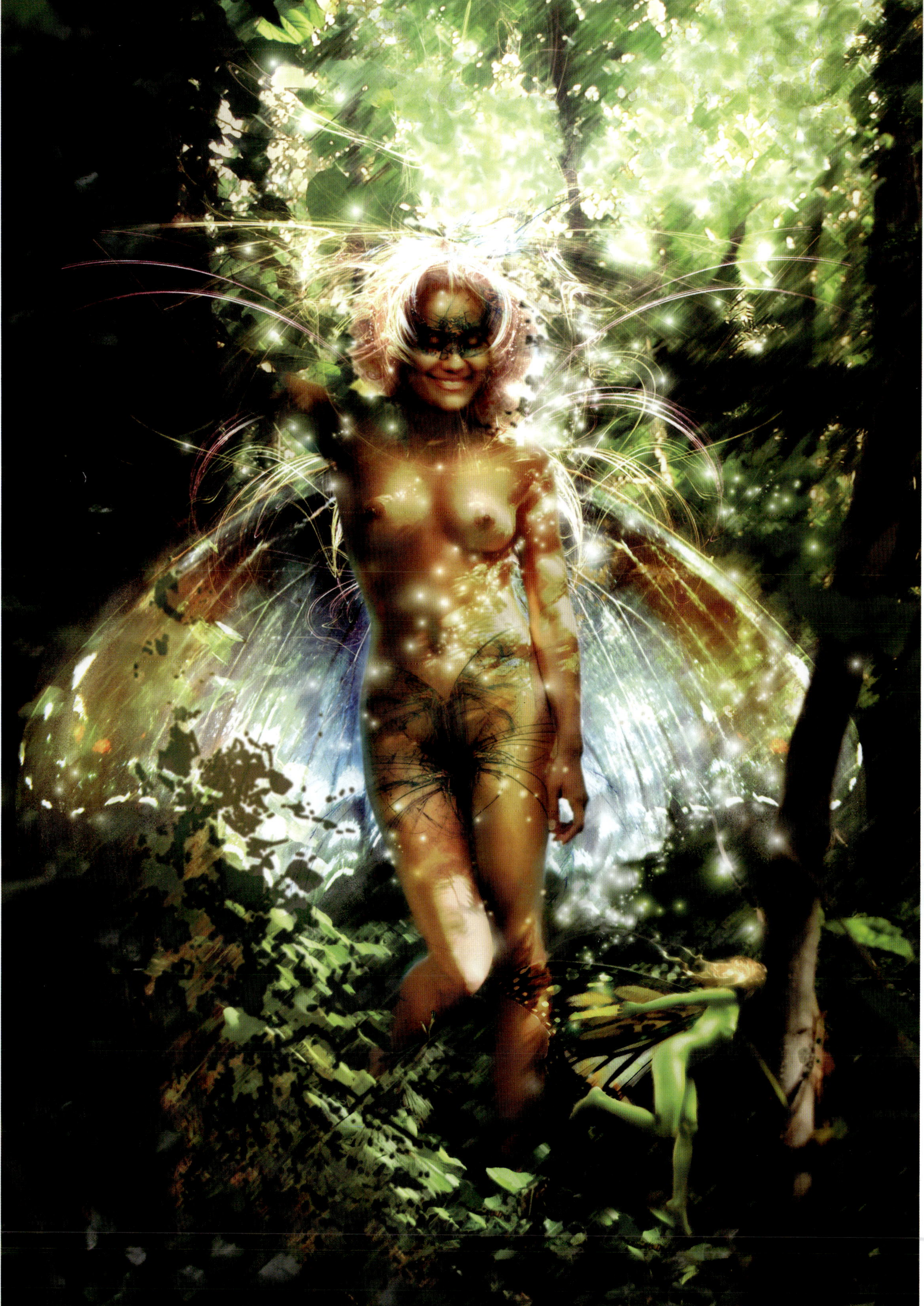

Just Before The Night

Digital: Photoshop/Painter

Some compositions are a struggle to make work. Others just fall into place. The relationship between the shapes in this piece made it click but it's the lighting idea that makes it dramatic. Every good painting starts with a good lighting idea. I can't remember who told me that because every mentor I've ever had have said it in one-way or another .
This piece uses several painting theories. Besides the obvious centered glow (light against dark) I applied one of my favorite color schemes, warm against cool.
By playing opposite colors against each other, in this case orange and blue, I've created a "complimentary" color scheme. It's one way to make the subject pop out.

Below is a poem inspired by my own artwork. Is that narcissism?

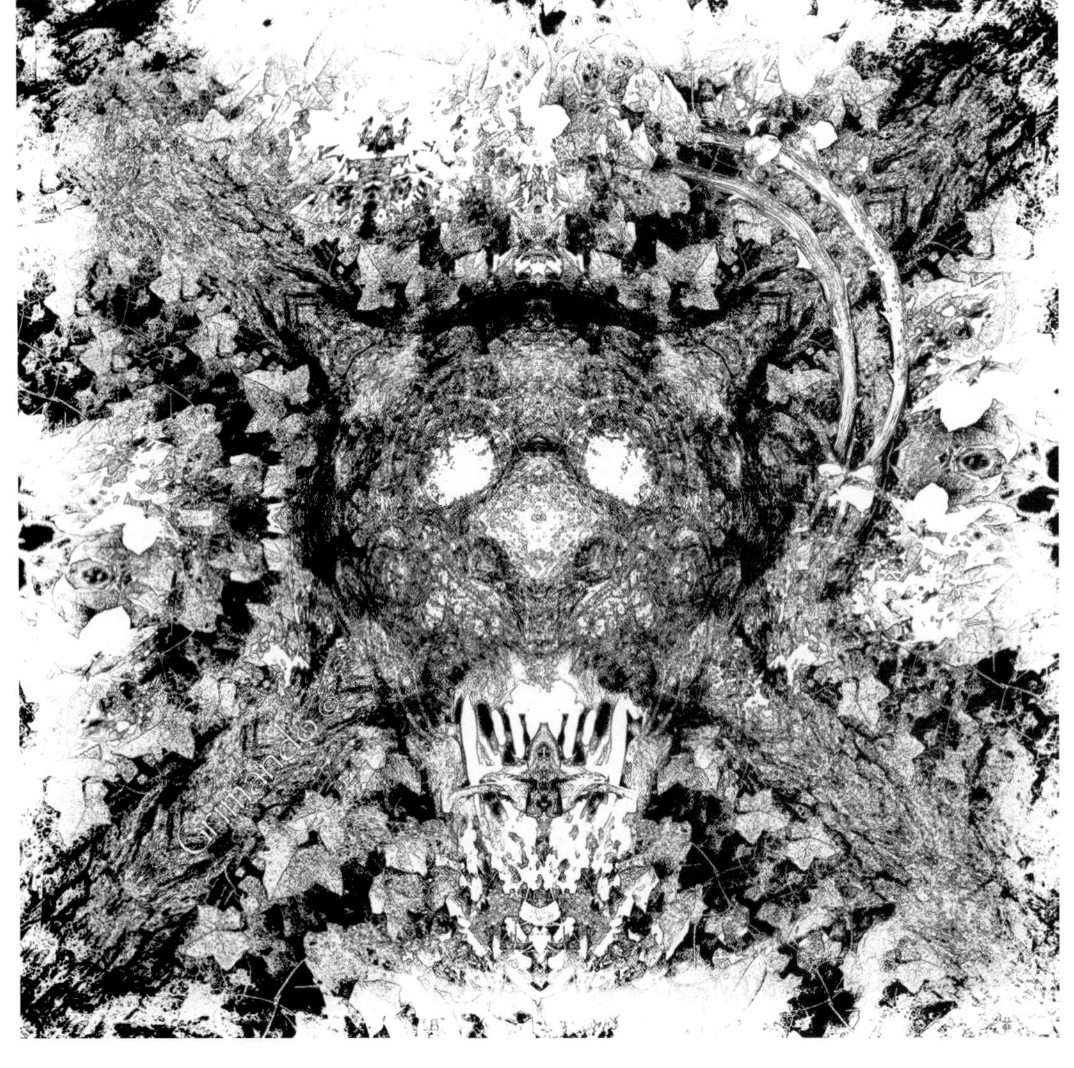

Just Before the Night

by Scott Grimando

Just Before the Night
I Awaken to the Site
Of Your Eerie Glow
And Our Dream of Flight

Magic Lives in Twilight
Hidden by the Day
Is the Sacred Path
Of the Timeless Way

Ancient Shadows Stir
And Ageless Beings
Pass Through Veils
That Separate Our Worlds

This is Your Right
And I Have Found a Way
To Live in Darkness
Guided By Your Light

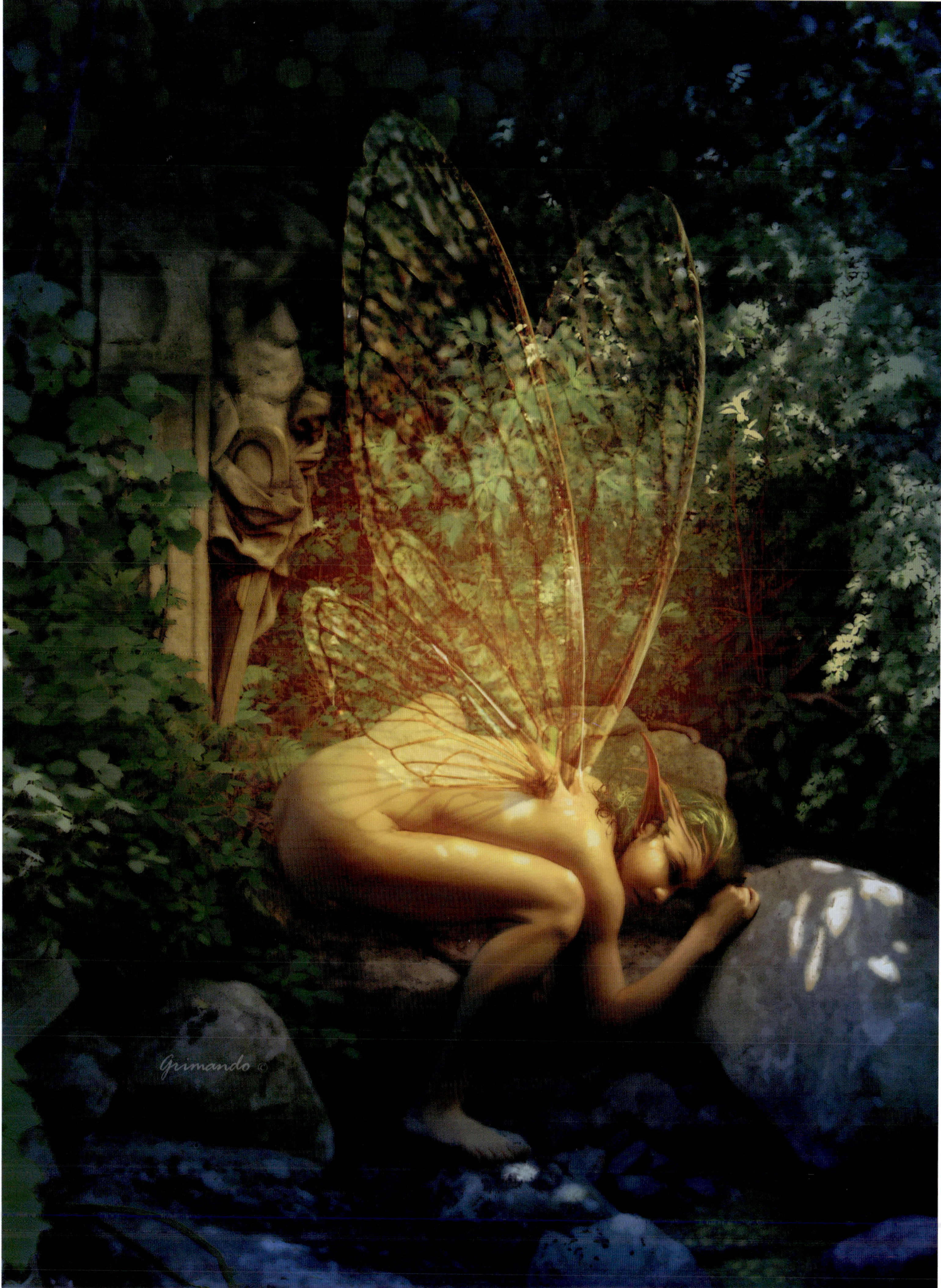
Grimando ©

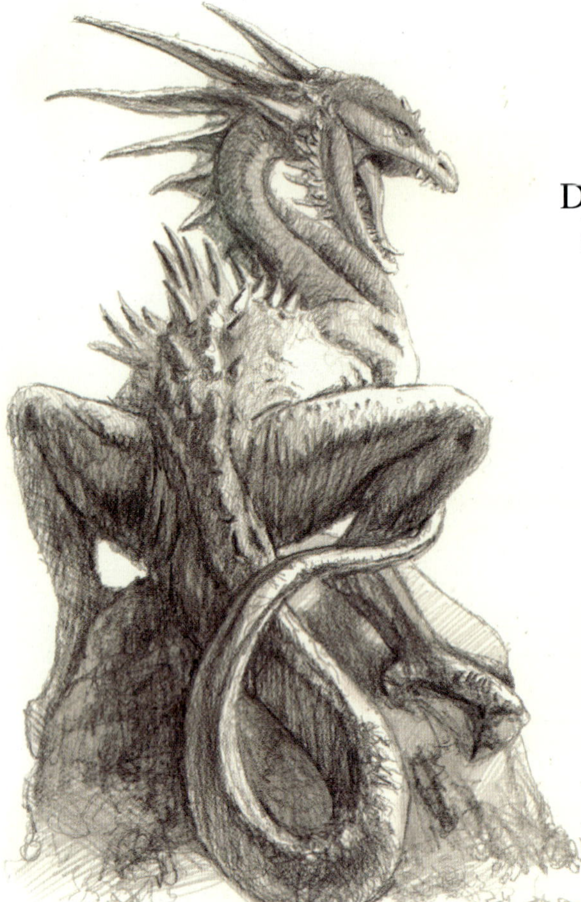

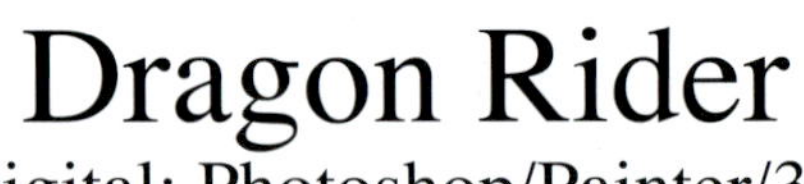

Dragon Rider

Digital: Photoshop/Painter/3D

For the love of dragons.
Dragon illustrations are immensely time consuming and at the same time irresistible. The universality of the myth captures everyone's imagination.
The tricky part of painting a convincing dragon is achieving realistic anatomy. Since they don't exist an artist must base them on other animals. The wings are easily based on bat wings. The head can be based on any reptile or amphibian. The body can range from gators to meerkats to rooster feet. What starts out as a cool little sketch becomes a big project when you try and flush out a fully realized mythical beast.

Walkabout

Analog Science Fiction Magazine Cover
Digital: Photoshop/Painter/3D

For the love of design.
Like the architecture in Dragon Rider I try and create my own unique design aesthetic for my 3D vehicles. Usually I start with a quick sketch inspired by something that catches my interest. I wanted this design to look like a big walking eyeball.
It's all-consuming when I start getting into the details. I'll lose track of time when working on a 3D design.
I have to make them look like they could really work.
The distinct advantage to designing in 3D is that I can view it from any angle and light it however I want.

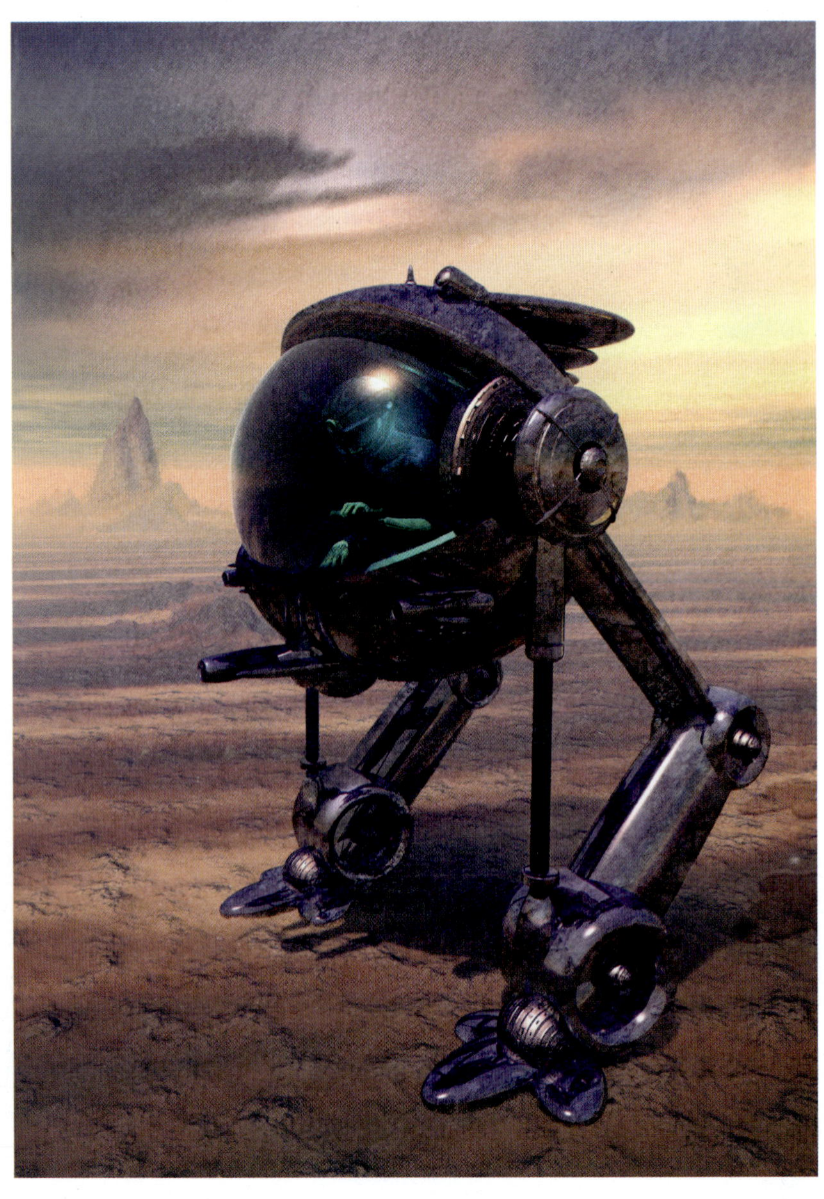

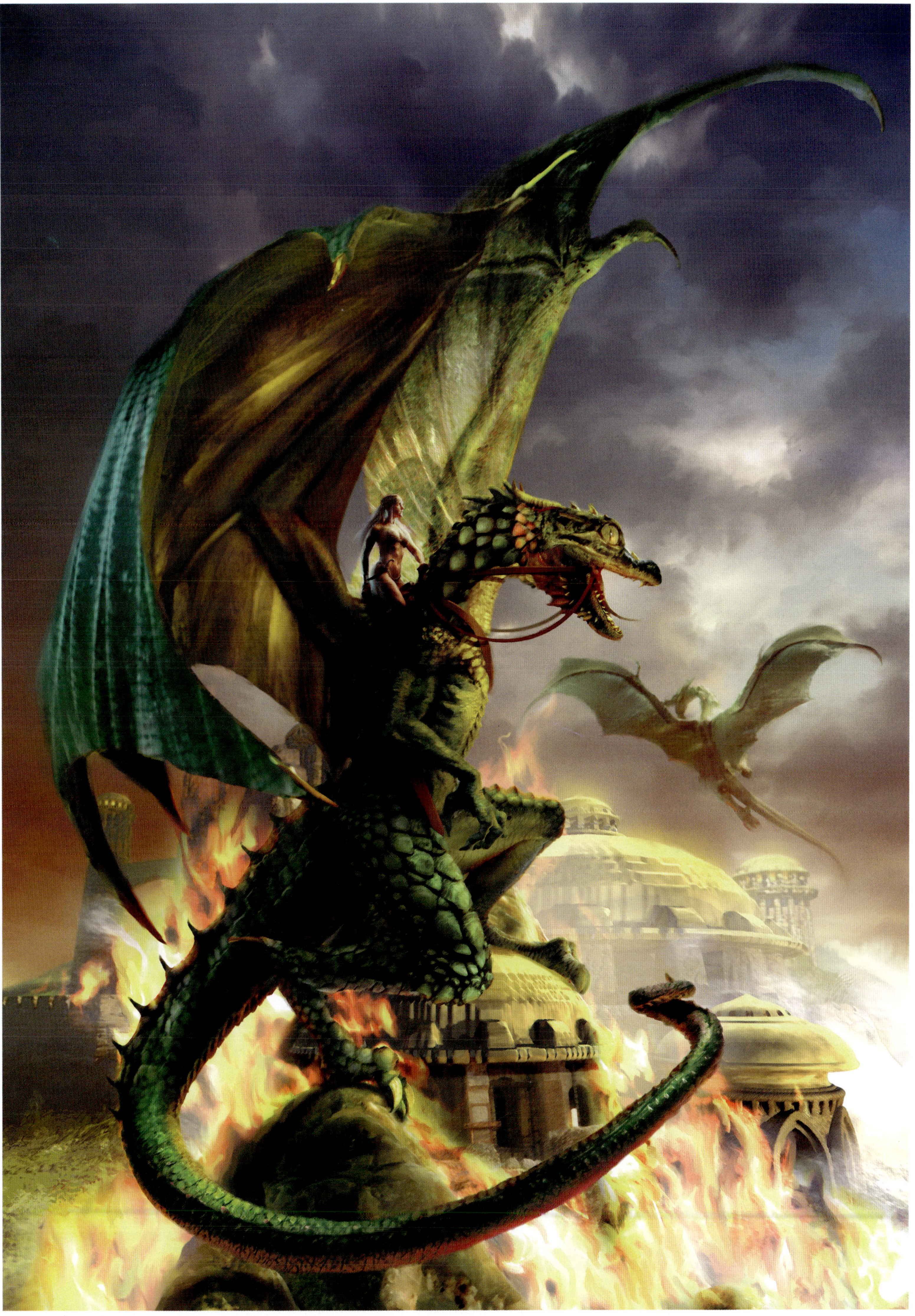

Between The Spaces

Poem Illustration
Digital: Photoshop/Painter

Part of what I try to achieve with my fairy work is an appreciation for the natural world around us. This idea of "between the spaces" came to me as I was looking out of a sub-basement window of my first studio onto the grass at ground level. I saw a myriad of insects going about their daily lives beneath the feet of the human world. They had jobs to do and conflicts every few inches. They had obstacles to overcome along the way but we don't see that because we don't look. There are worlds within worlds if you care to look close enough.

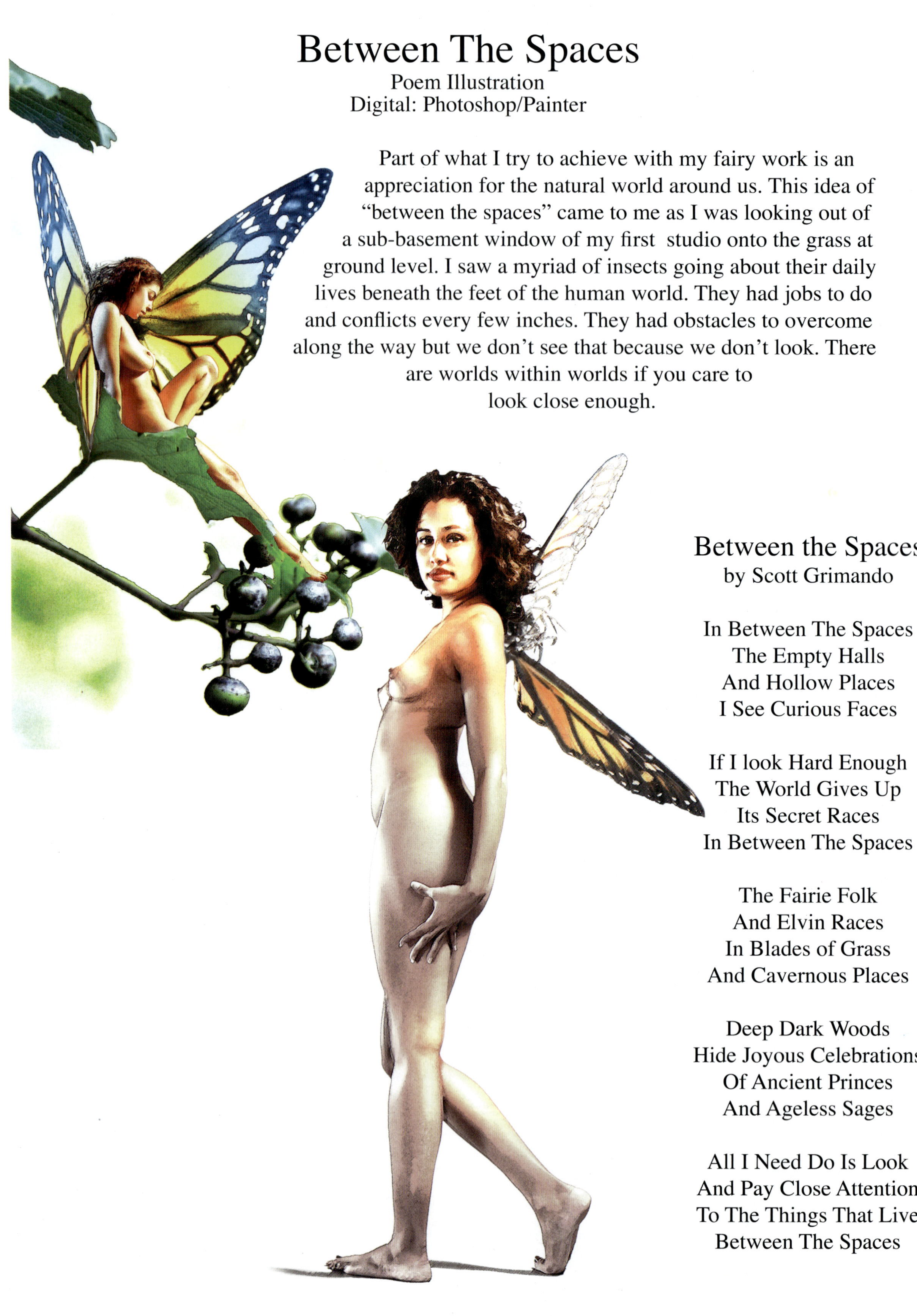

Between the Spaces
by Scott Grimando

In Between The Spaces
The Empty Halls
And Hollow Places
I See Curious Faces

If I look Hard Enough
The World Gives Up
Its Secret Races
In Between The Spaces

The Fairie Folk
And Elvin Races
In Blades of Grass
And Cavernous Places

Deep Dark Woods
Hide Joyous Celebrations
Of Ancient Princes
And Ageless Sages

All I Need Do Is Look
And Pay Close Attention
To The Things That Live
Between The Spaces

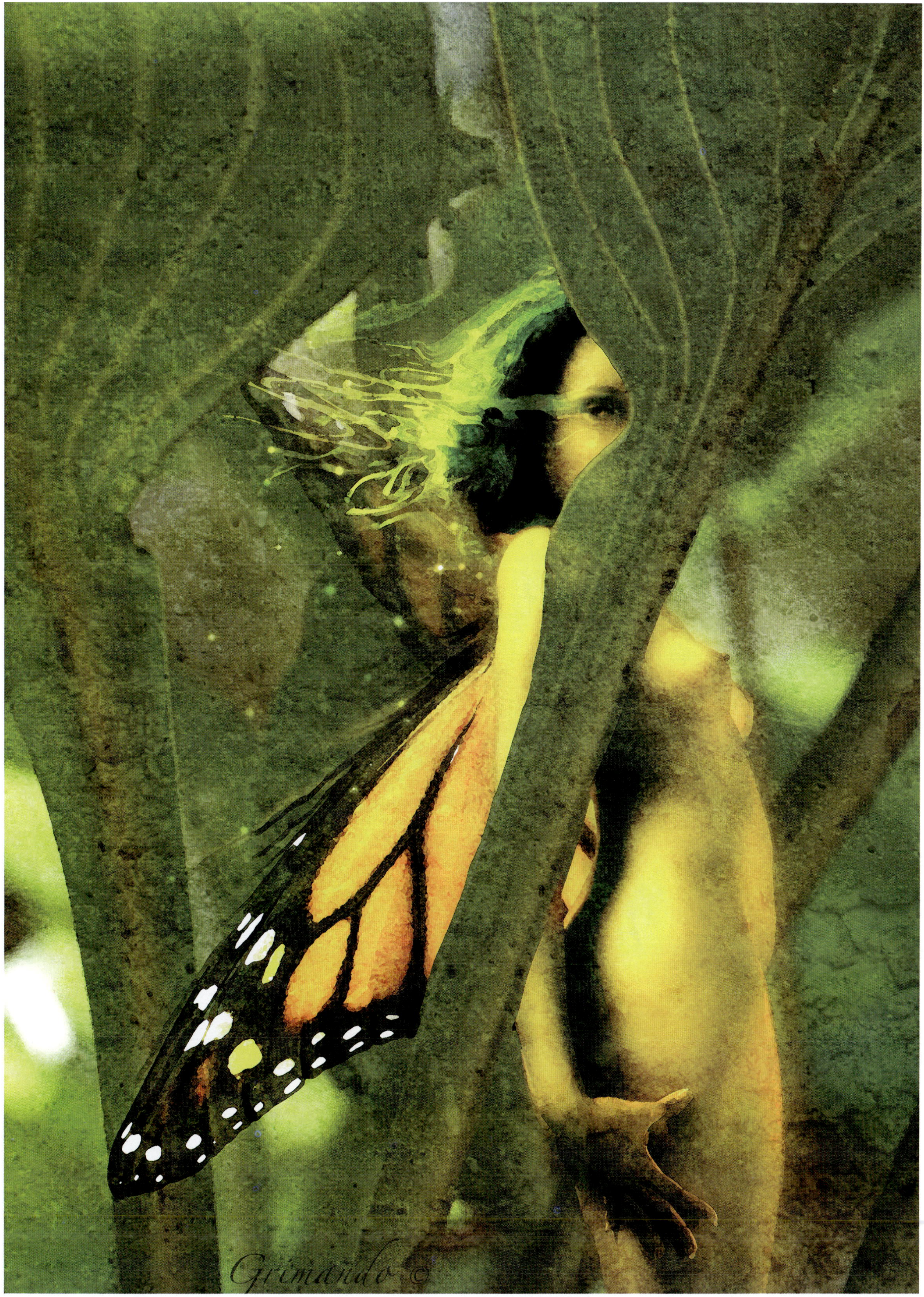
Grimando ©

The Grail

Digital: Photoshop/Painter/3D

I've always had a soft spot for the Arthurian legends and the Knights of the Round Table. It's one of the mythologies that permeate our art and media. There have been countless movies and books that use or are influenced by this rich body of medieval literature. What has always appealed to me (besides Excalibur) is the druid undertones. Merlin and Morgan le Fay represented the old Earth-based religions. The heathen mysticism that Christianity both feared and idealized for its knowledge.

In this piece I'm representing Morgan le Fay as integrally bound to the Earth. She tempts a knight with a false grail. The true grail represents knowledge and the power to remake the world in the new God's image. The false grail represents temptation and death. This is of course my own interpretation of this intricate and complex legend.

There's been a lot of recent research done on the true origins of the Arthurian Legends. While I find the research interesting this legend loses its intrigue and romance if it's taken too literally.

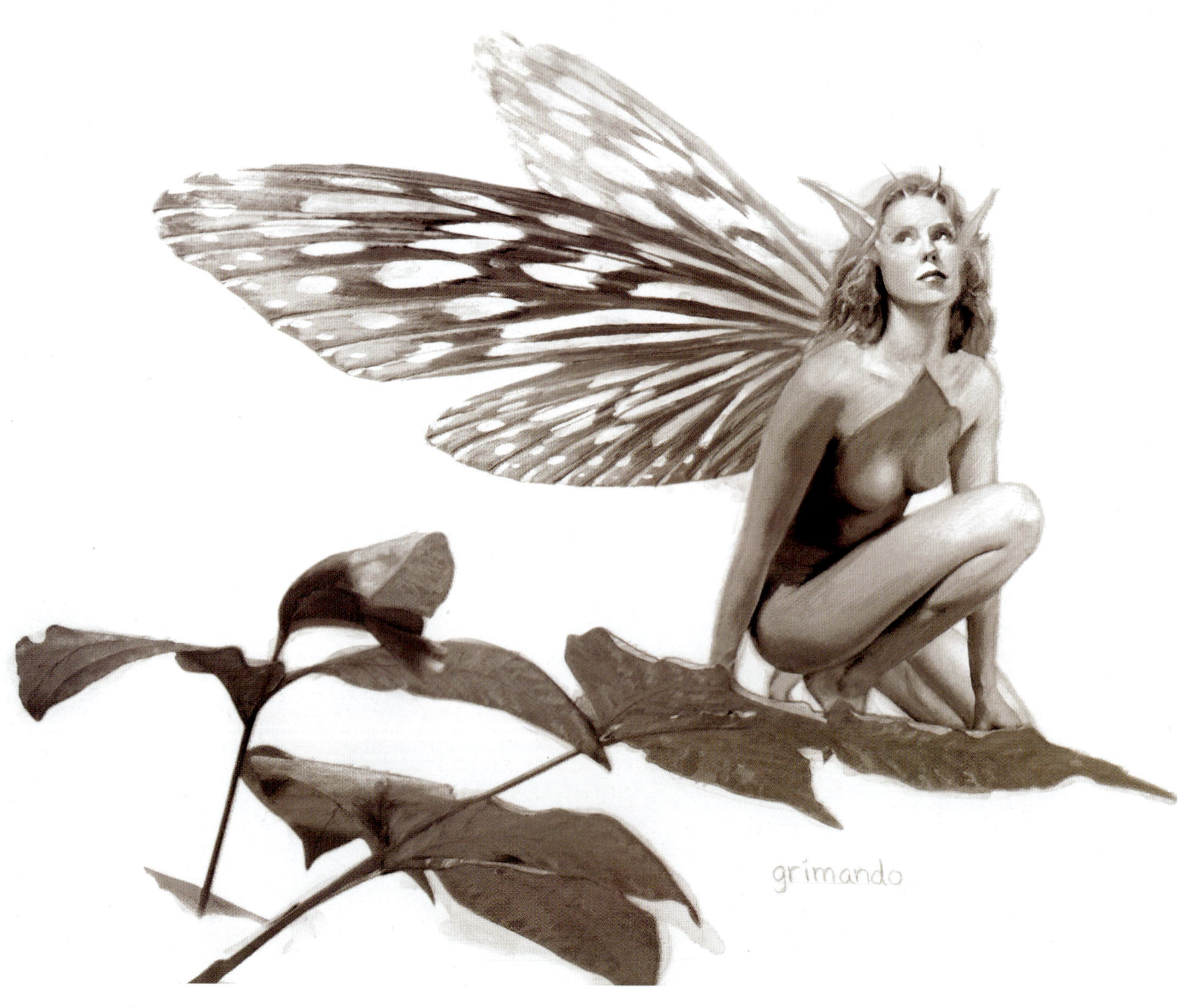

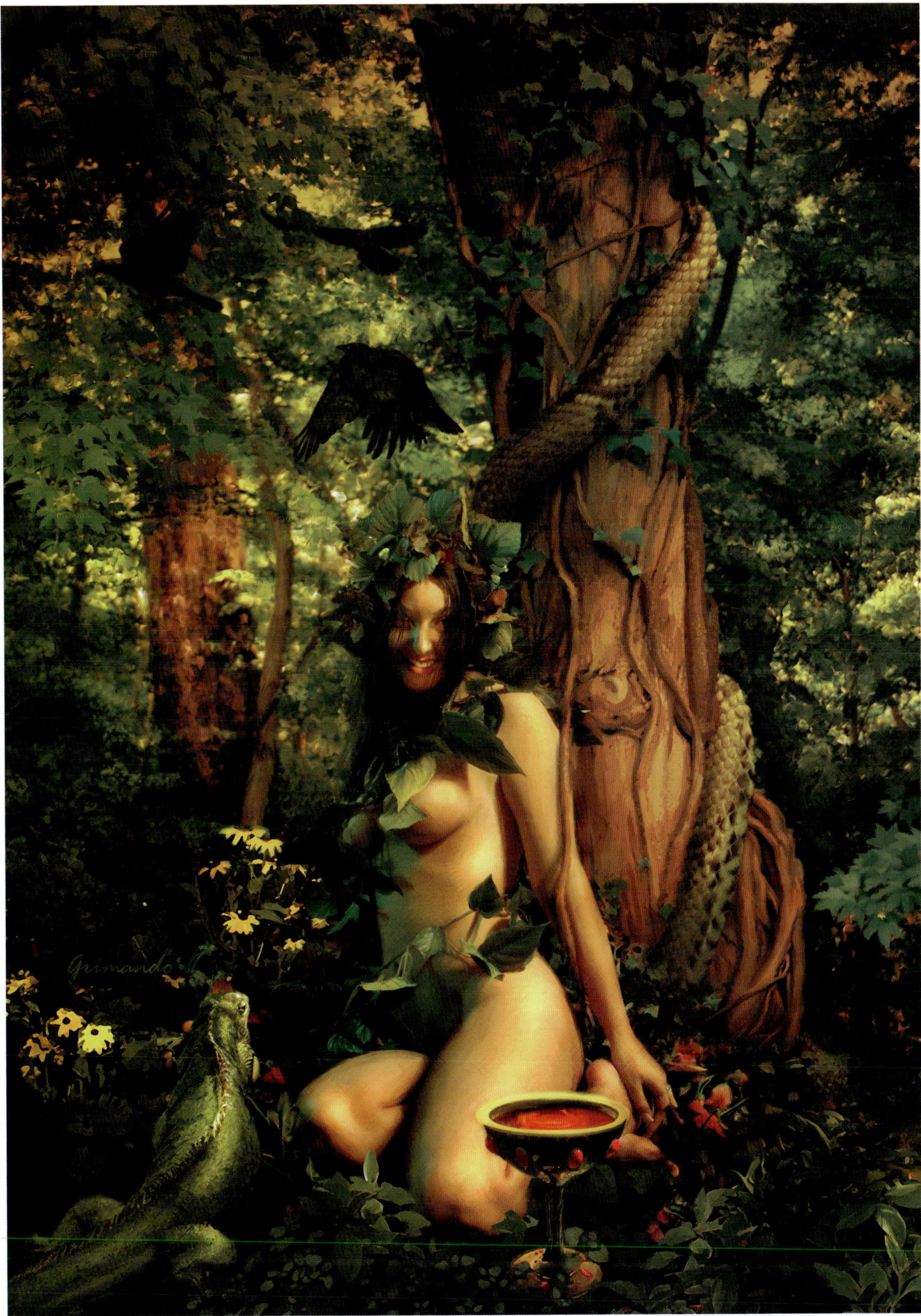
Grimando

Gestation

Personal Story Illustration
Digital: Photoshop/3D

Gestation (or Egg) is an idea I've been toying with for a long time. Several years ago I wrote a science fiction story about a future where women have been wiped out by a plague along with much of the male population. Sex slaves are gestated in an egg chamber for the wealthy and powerful but they only have a life expectancy of about a year.
While this topic may seem sexist, the story examines important social issues.
I put off working on this first image because the 3D elements take a long time to model. By that I mean that each element has to be sculpted in a 3D program then textured and rendered to work with the live model reference.
I realized that I already had the elements modeled as bits and pieces of other illustrations so I put them together in this scene. I then lit and rendered it. That's the great thing about 3D, you can use models over and over again. Once they're repositioned, rotated, re-light and re-textured, they're not even recognizable.
After all the elements are in place, the real illustration begins.

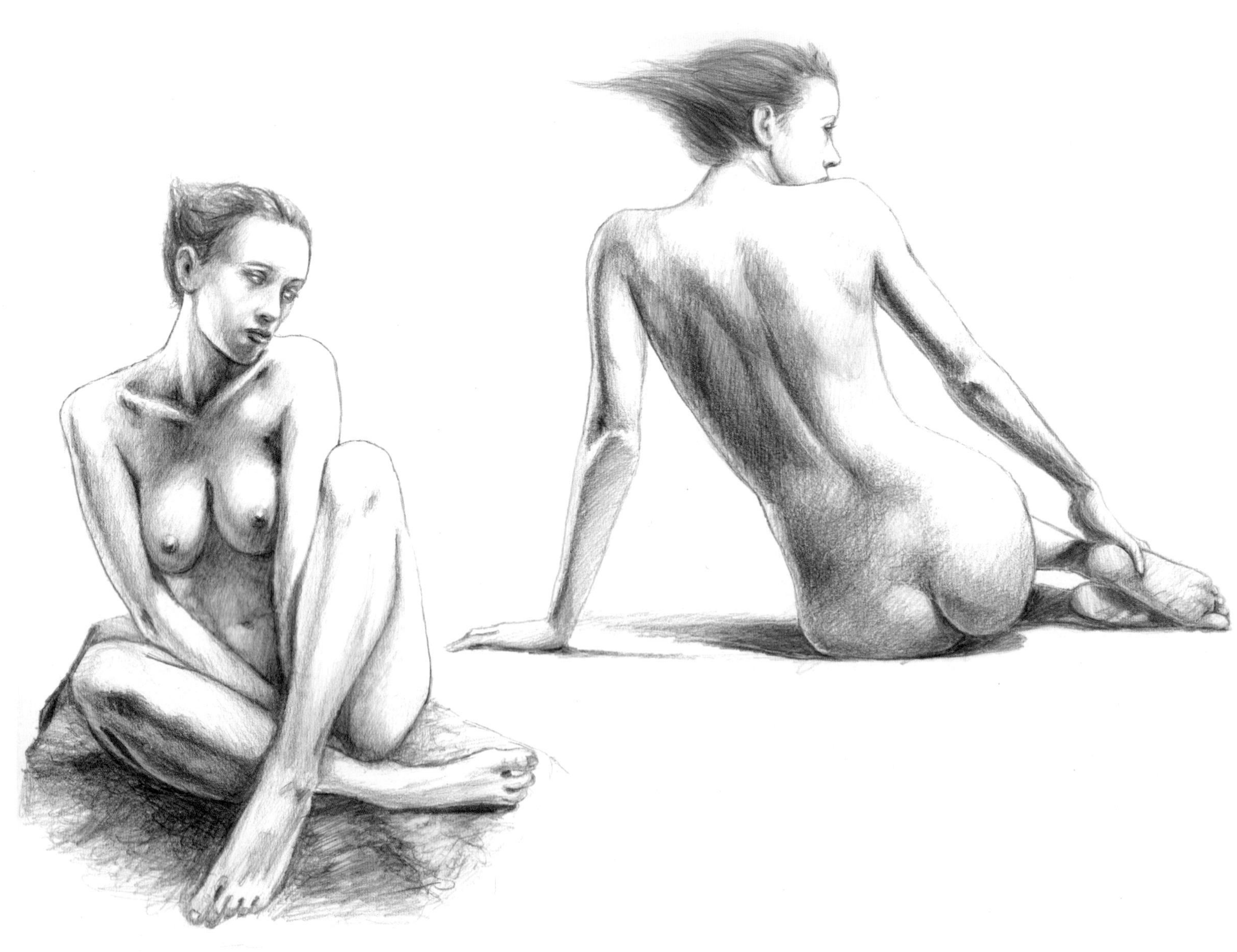

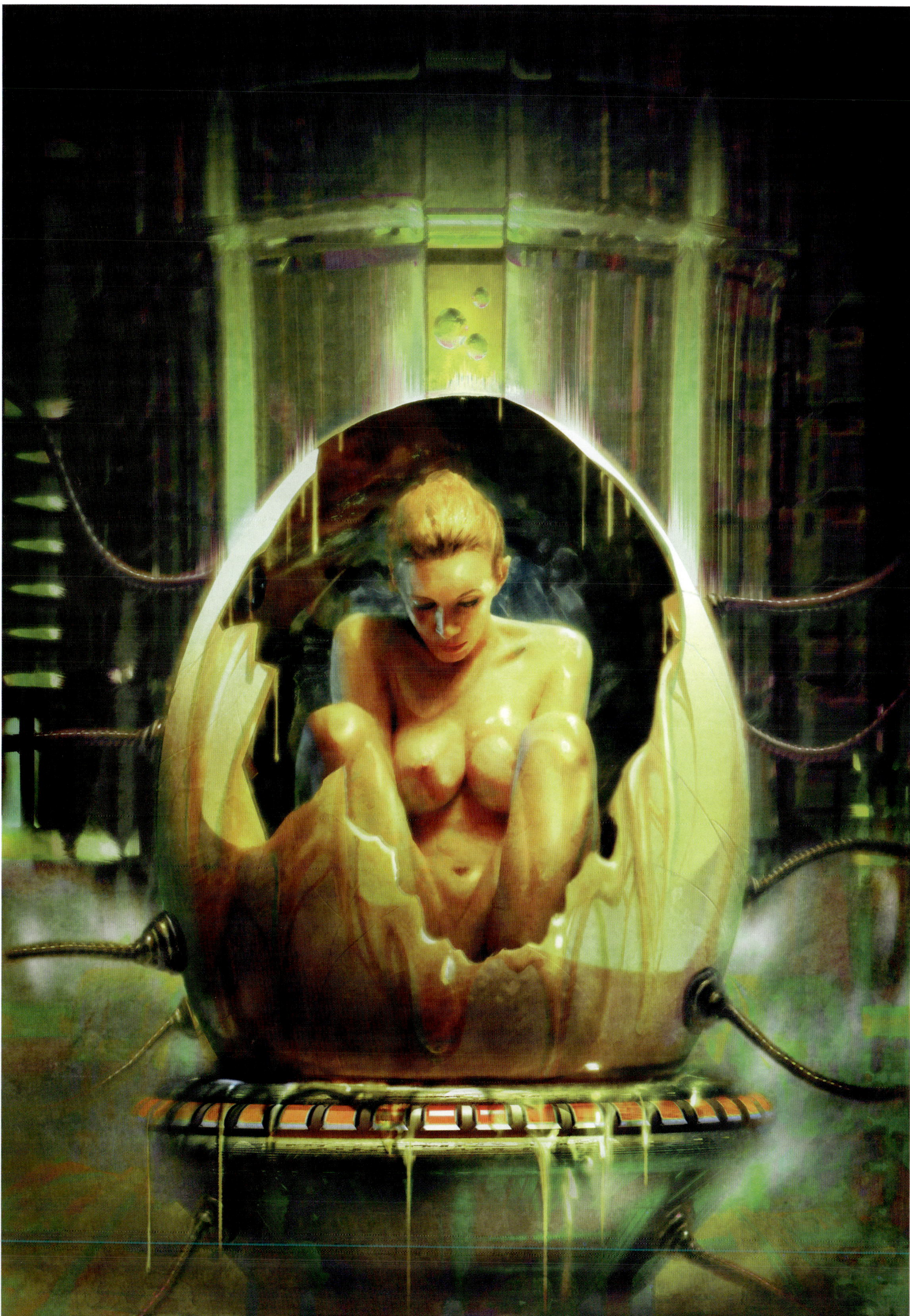

The Green Man

Poem Illustration
Digital: Photoshop/Painter

The Green Man is an important pagan myth that spreads through many cultures. He represents a guardian of nature and is a symbol of rebirth. I've often said that as myths slip away we must assume the responsibility for the gaps they leave. In this painting and poem I've tried to express the idea that our connection to the natural world is slipping away from us. As a piece of the Green Man floats down a stream a nude girl attempts to save it in a sense recapturing her innocence.

The Monarch Queen

Digital: Photoshop/Painter

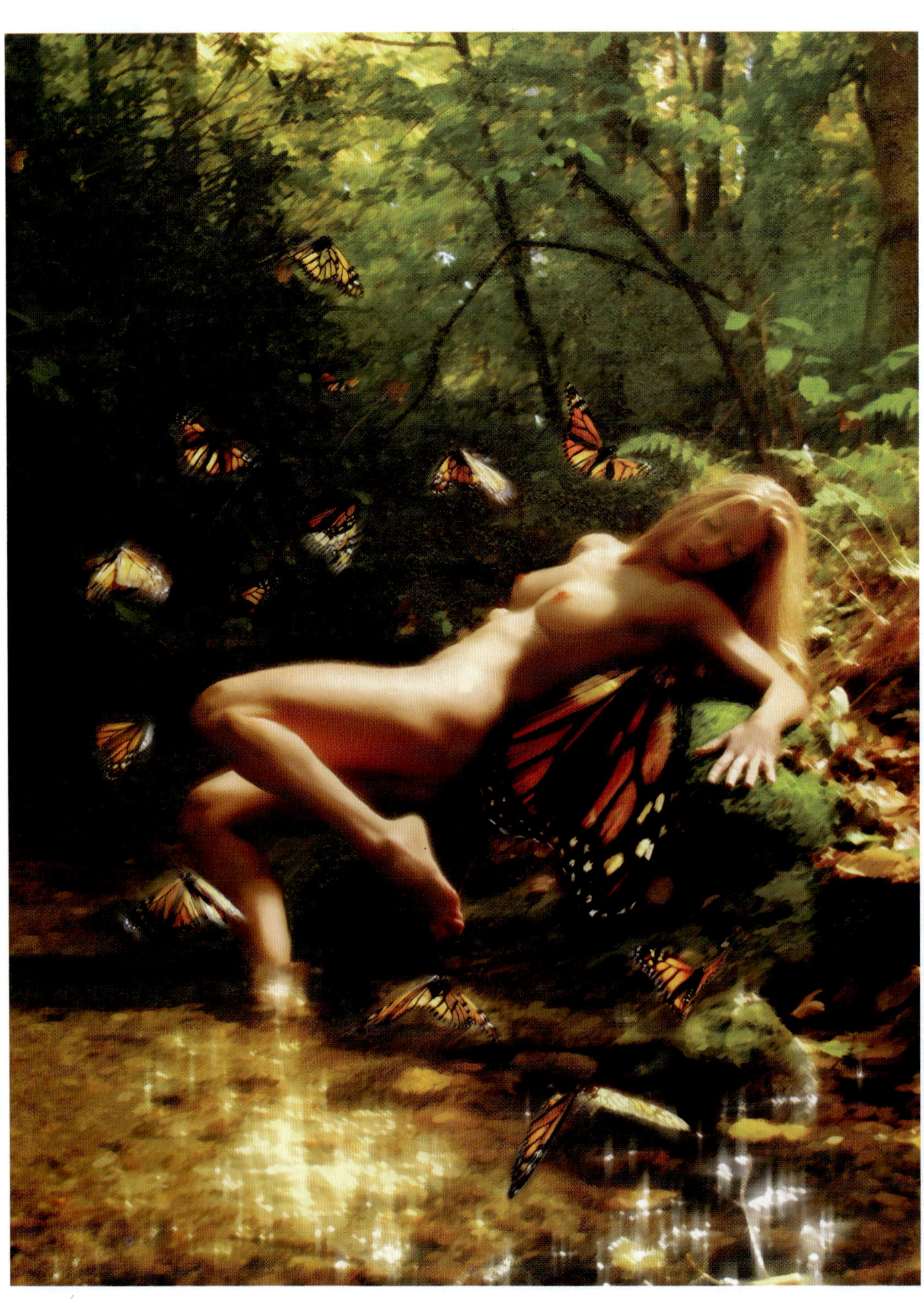

Leaves Are Masks

by Scott Grimando

Leaves are Masks
For the Oldest Ones
Spirits of Earth
Hidden From None

And For All They're Worth
We Do Not See
The Tree For Its Branches
And The Green Mans Glee

We Walk Beside Them
With Our Eyes Closed
Grasping at straws
Making Up Foes

We Make Our Stand
All The While
Plagued by Demons
Of Our Own Command

A Man is a Shadow
Of Forgotten Lands
A Beast of Legend
With Death In His Hands

The Great Contradiction
A Poet And Schemer
Lost in the Faith
Of His Own Conviction

The World is a Dream
Its Roots Dug Deep
With Singular Purpose
To Add to it's Strength

And the Trees Resolve
Is The Heart of the Forest
Withered And Dying
While Our Connection
Slowly Dissolves

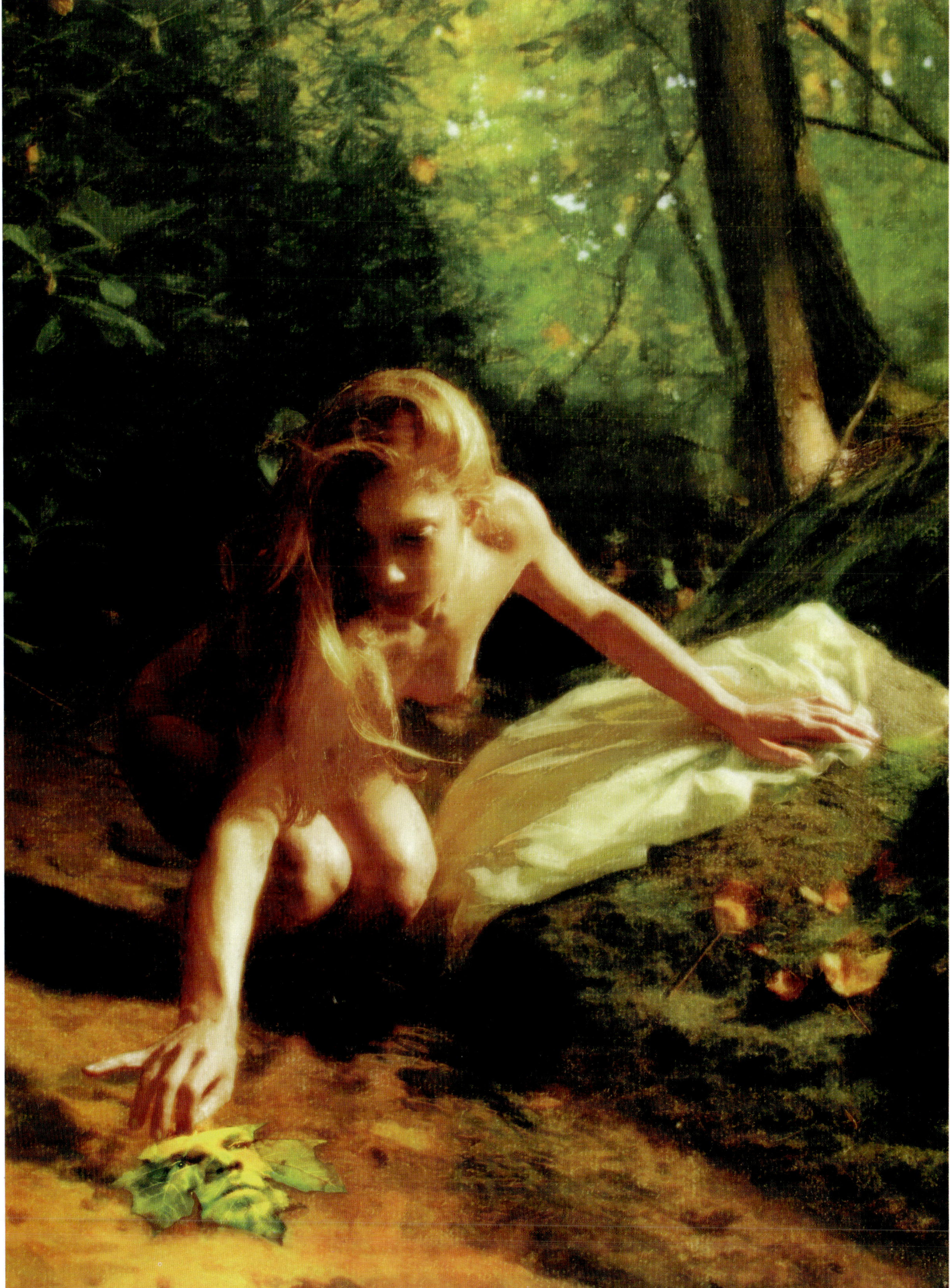

Fairy Tale

Wedding Invite
Digital: Photoshop/Painter/3D

This piece was my wedding invitation. My wife and I dressed up and posed for the illustration. It's the standard theme of the damsel in distress but with a distinctly modern twist. After going over the reference shots, we decided on a pose that showed a position of equality between us. She is drawing her dagger ready to fight back and the dragon is trying to grab my shield, so I'm in as much danger as she is.

One of the wedding guests commented how amazing it was that we were able to find two models that looked so much like us. LOL! Most people have no idea what goes into an illustration.

Another guest thought the wedding was going to take place in a castle because I had a painting of a fantasy castle on the back of the invitation.

I couldn't help but think, "does she think that castle actually exists"?

Sea Serpent/Doomed

Inquest Magazine Spread
Digital: Photoshop/Painter/3D

Dragons are a universal myth and every culture has their own stories. Being a fisherman and boater, I've always been drawn to the myth of the sea serpents.

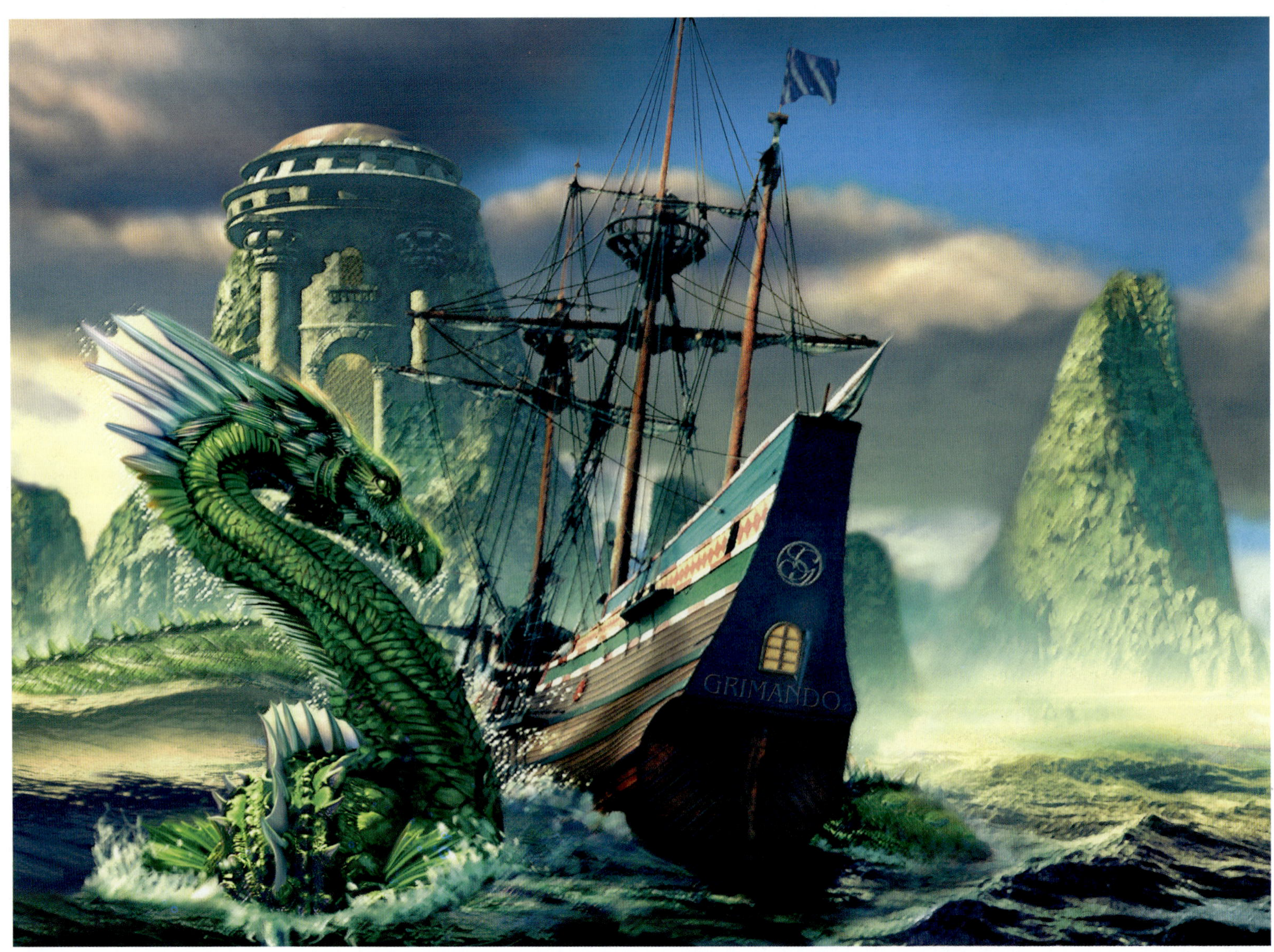

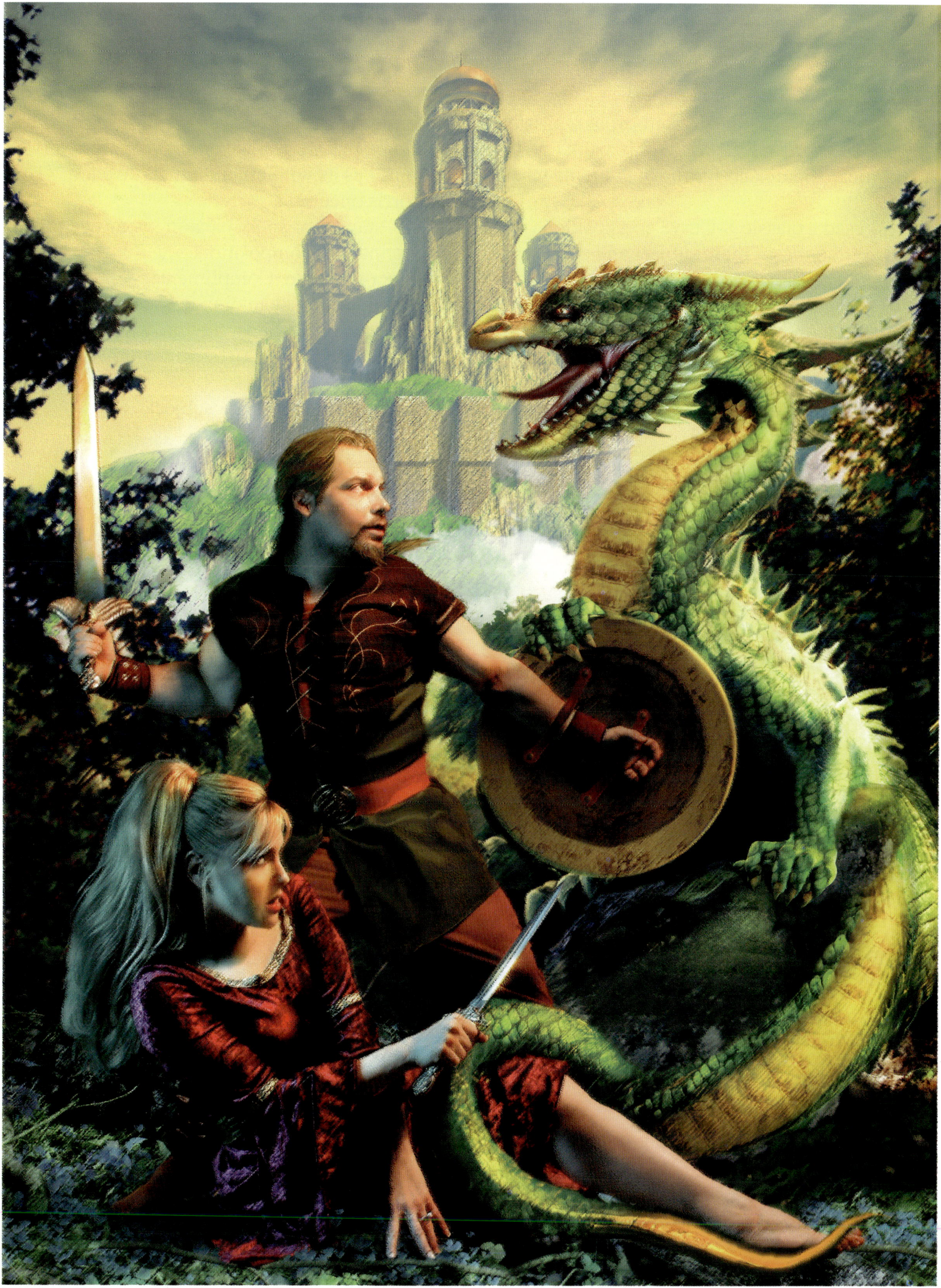

The Fairy Stream

Oils on Masonite
24" x 36"

Many of these fairy pieces start off as a passion for the figure reference I'm using. I'm fascinated by the human form and if I could only paint one thing it would be that. It's so naked in its expression. By that I mean there is no fur to cover up the tension of the muscles as with other animals. We are, "The Naked Ape", as Desmond Morris once said.

Here I used a classic S-Curve composition (in this case "S" stands for snake) leading your eye to the main subject and at the same time deep into the composition.

The complimentary color schemes help to direct your eye. Complimentary color schemes aren't as simple as using opposites such as a blue against an orange. There is a degree of subtlety to the application. In other words I used a muted blue/gray against the fairly intense orange of the figure. The flowers in the foreground are also a more intense red against green contrast near the figure then towards the edge.

Everything in the composition should lead your eye to the main subject.

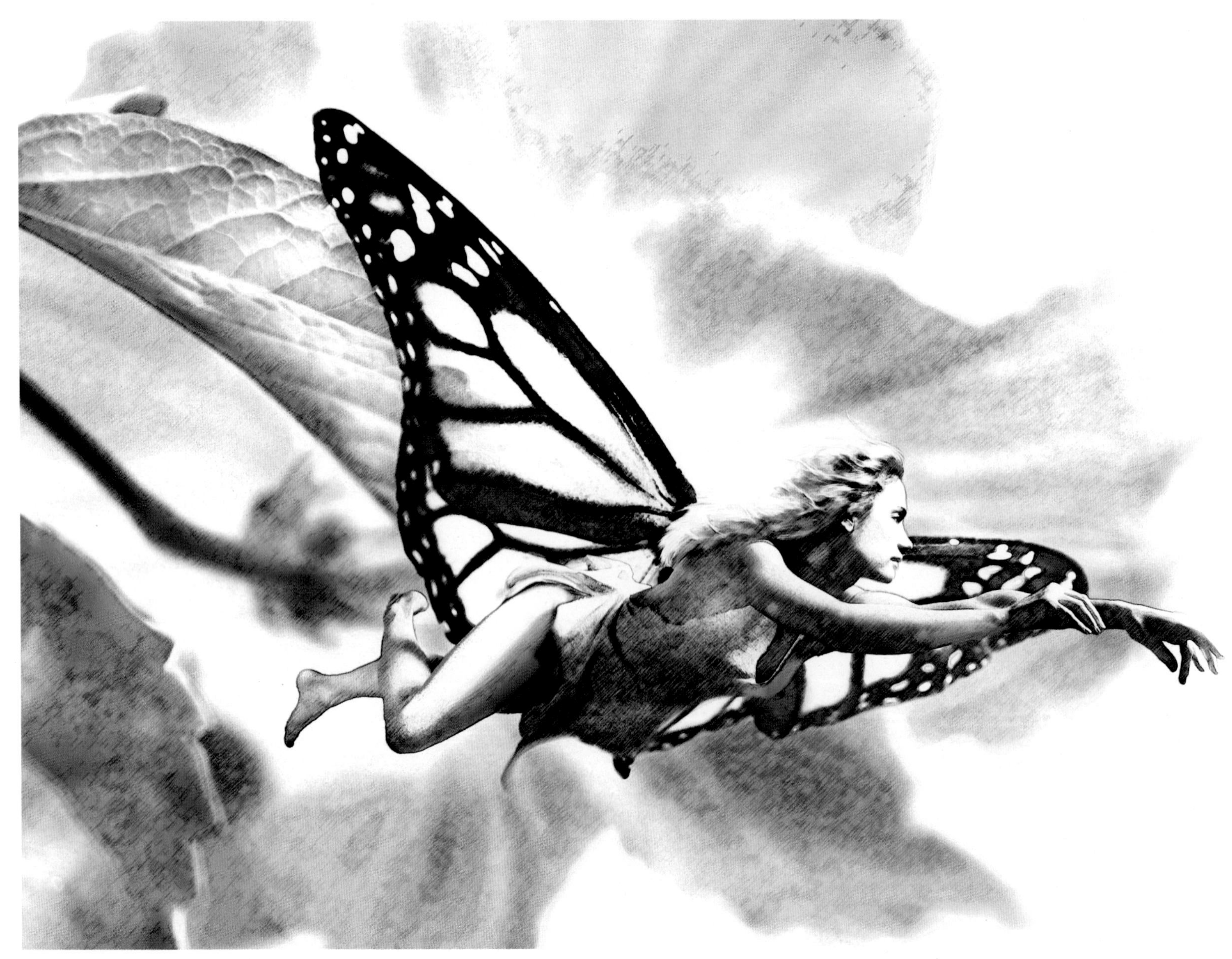

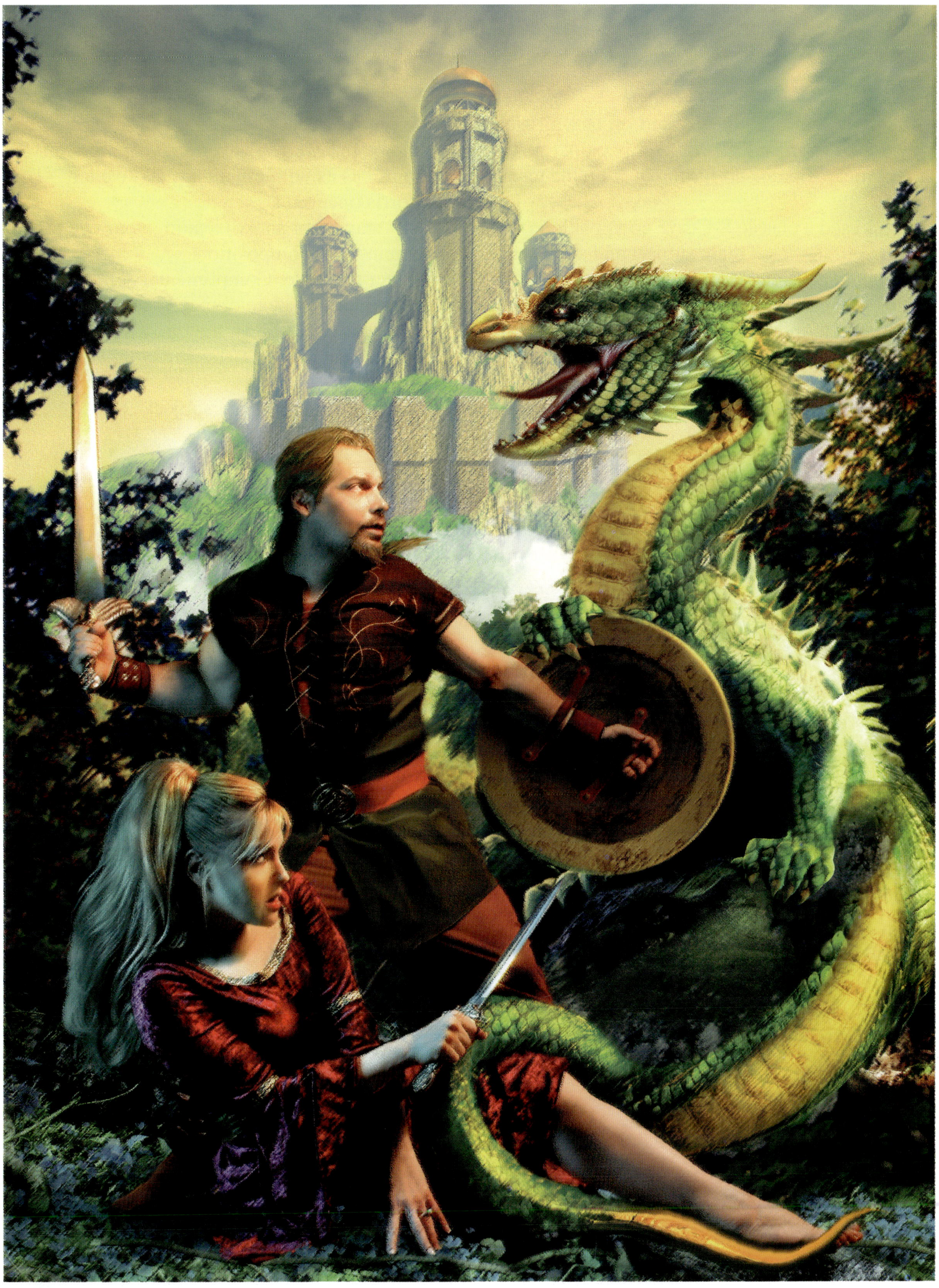

The Fairy Stream

Oils on Masonite
24" x 36"

Many of these fairy pieces start off as a passion for the figure reference I'm using. I'm fascinated by the human form and if I could only paint one thing it would be that. It's so naked in its expression. By that I mean there is no fur to cover up the tension of the muscles as with other animals. We are, "The Naked Ape", as Desmond Morris once said.

Here I used a classic S-Curve composition (in this case "S" stands for snake) leading your eye to the main subject and at the same time deep into the composition.

The complimentary color schemes help to direct your eye. Complimentary color schemes aren't as simple as using opposites such as a blue against an orange. There is a degree of subtlety to the application. In other words I used a muted blue/gray against the fairly intense orange of the figure. The flowers in the foreground are also a more intense red against green contrast near the figure then towards the edge.

Everything in the composition should lead your eye to the main subject.

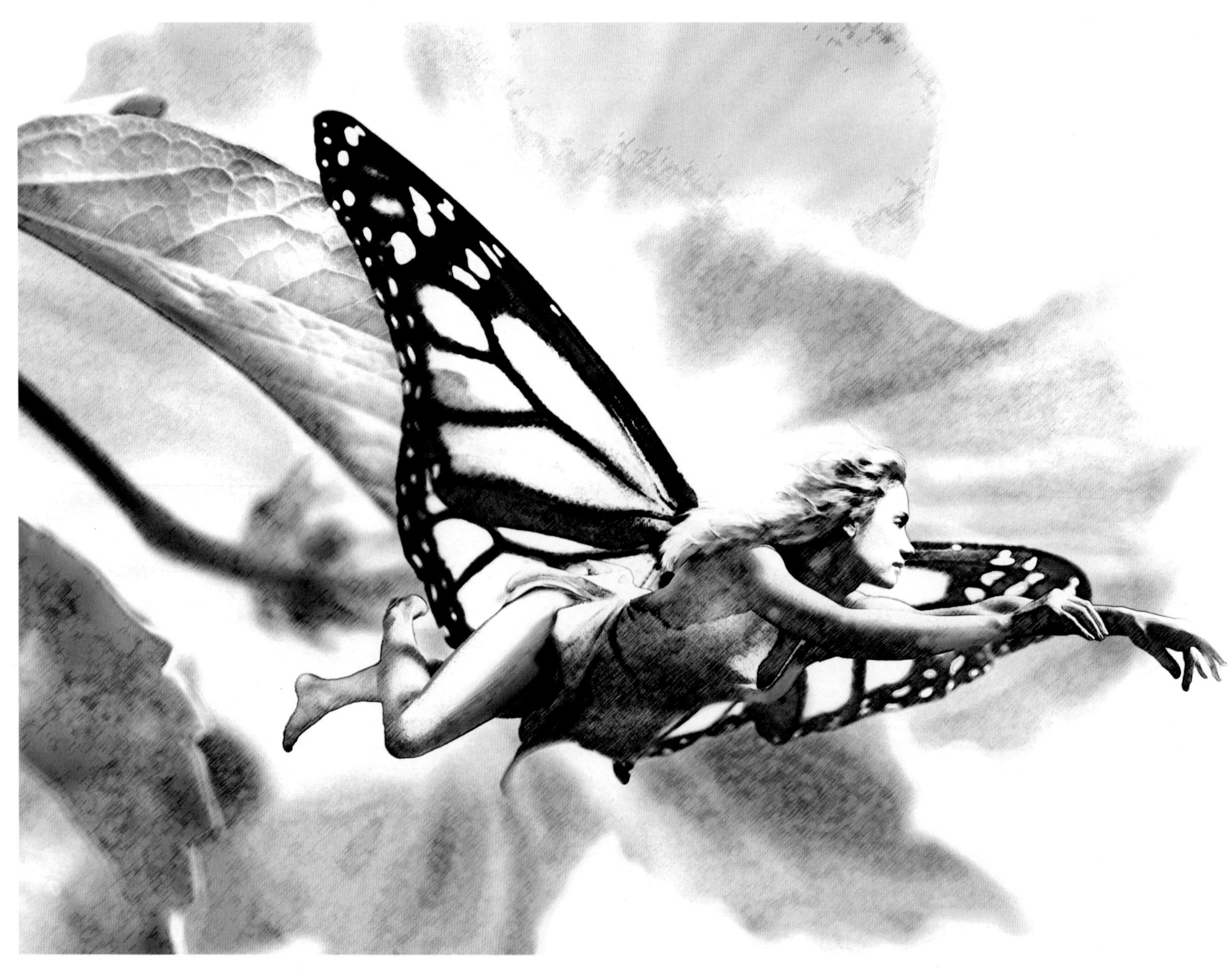

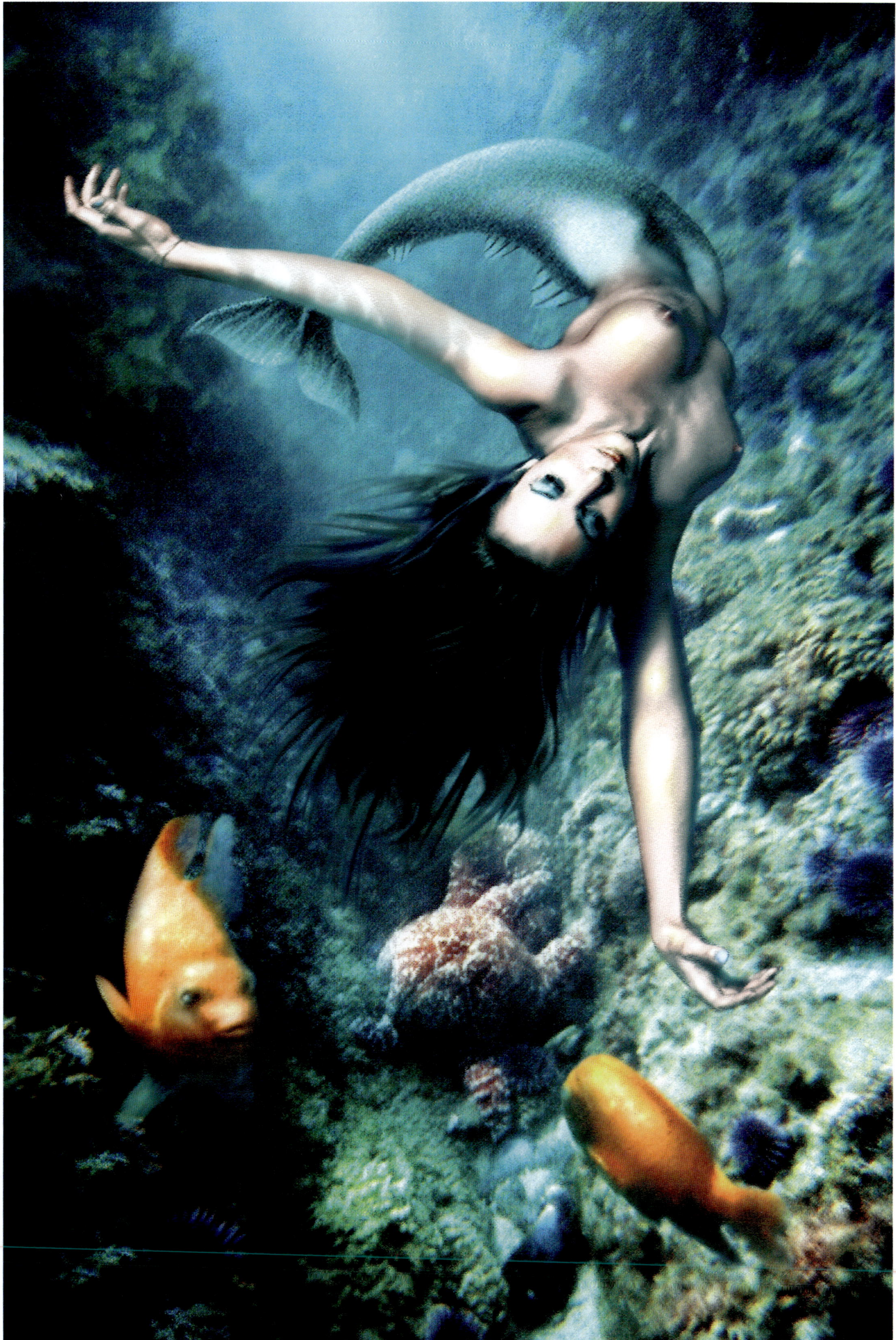

The Orb of Truth

Digital: Photoshop/Painter

This was my preferred pose for the Gilfeather cover. If the art director had liked it I would have added the ship and islands behind her.
As it turned out I got another nice illustration out of it.

Below is an early Photoshop sample of mine that doesn't really have a name but I like to call it, The Devil In Her. I was just experimenting with layer and paint effects. This one just feels right even after all these years.

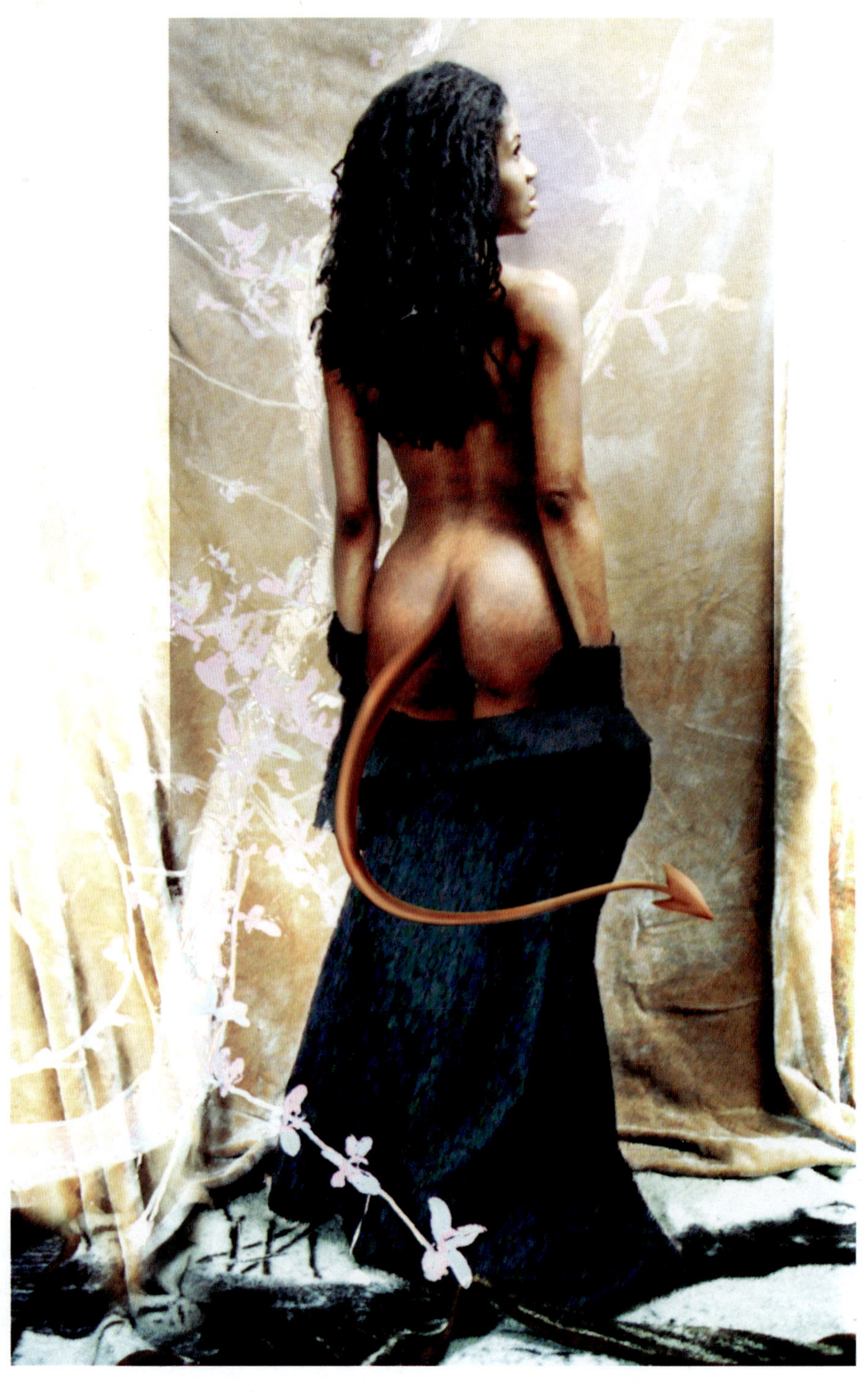

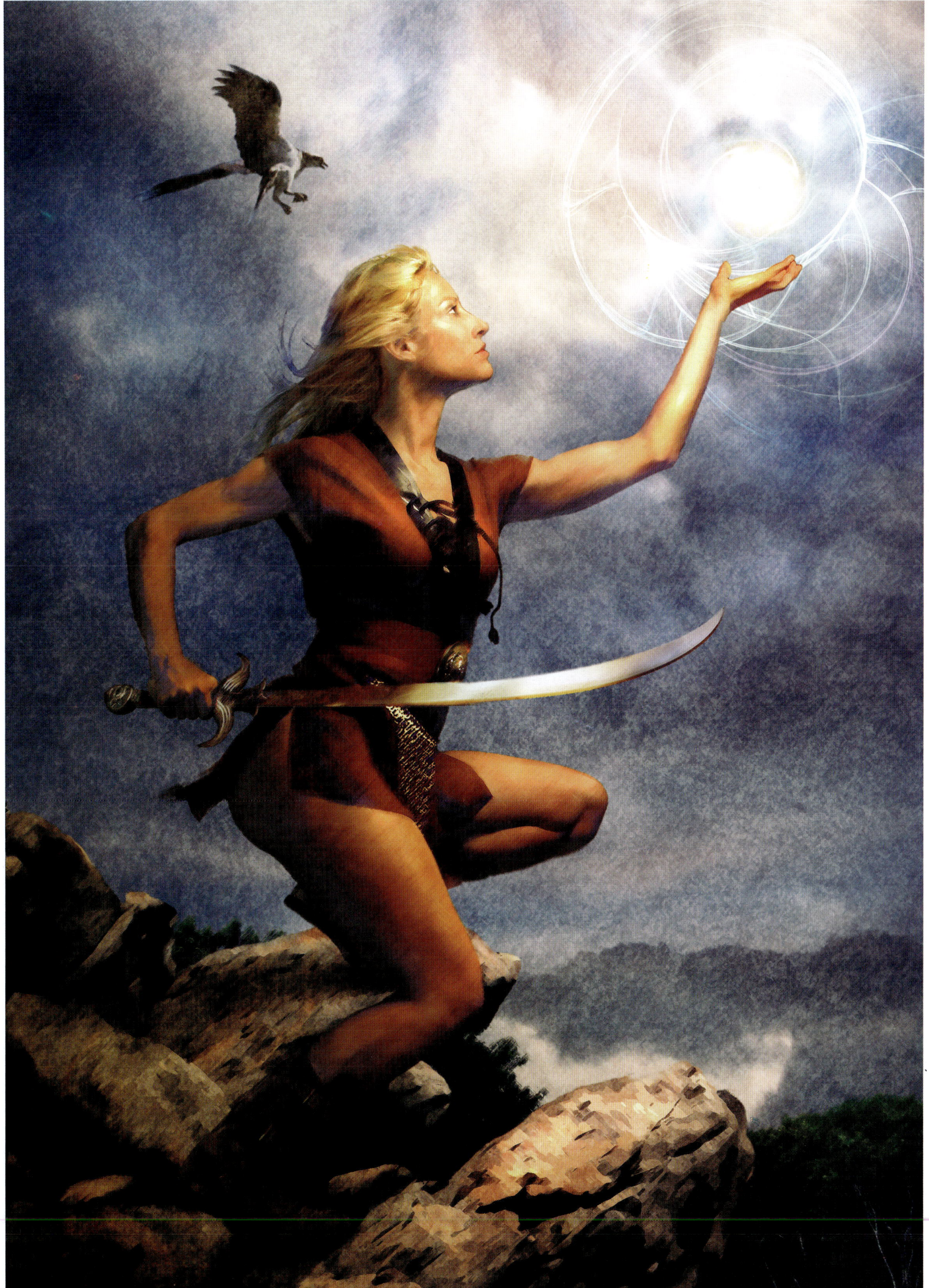

Dorin's Bane

Digital: Photoshop/Painter/3D

As much as I hate to admit it, there are some differences between illustration and fine art. The difference is that fine art does not necessarily have to tell a story. Fine art can just be a pretty picture. Illustration is much more difficult because the artist has to convey an idea. The viewer must be drawn into the narrative and ask themselves, what's going on in this picture?

Spines 1

Digital: Photoshop/Painter

This is a recurring theme in my figure work. I like the way the subtle spines make the viewer do a double take.

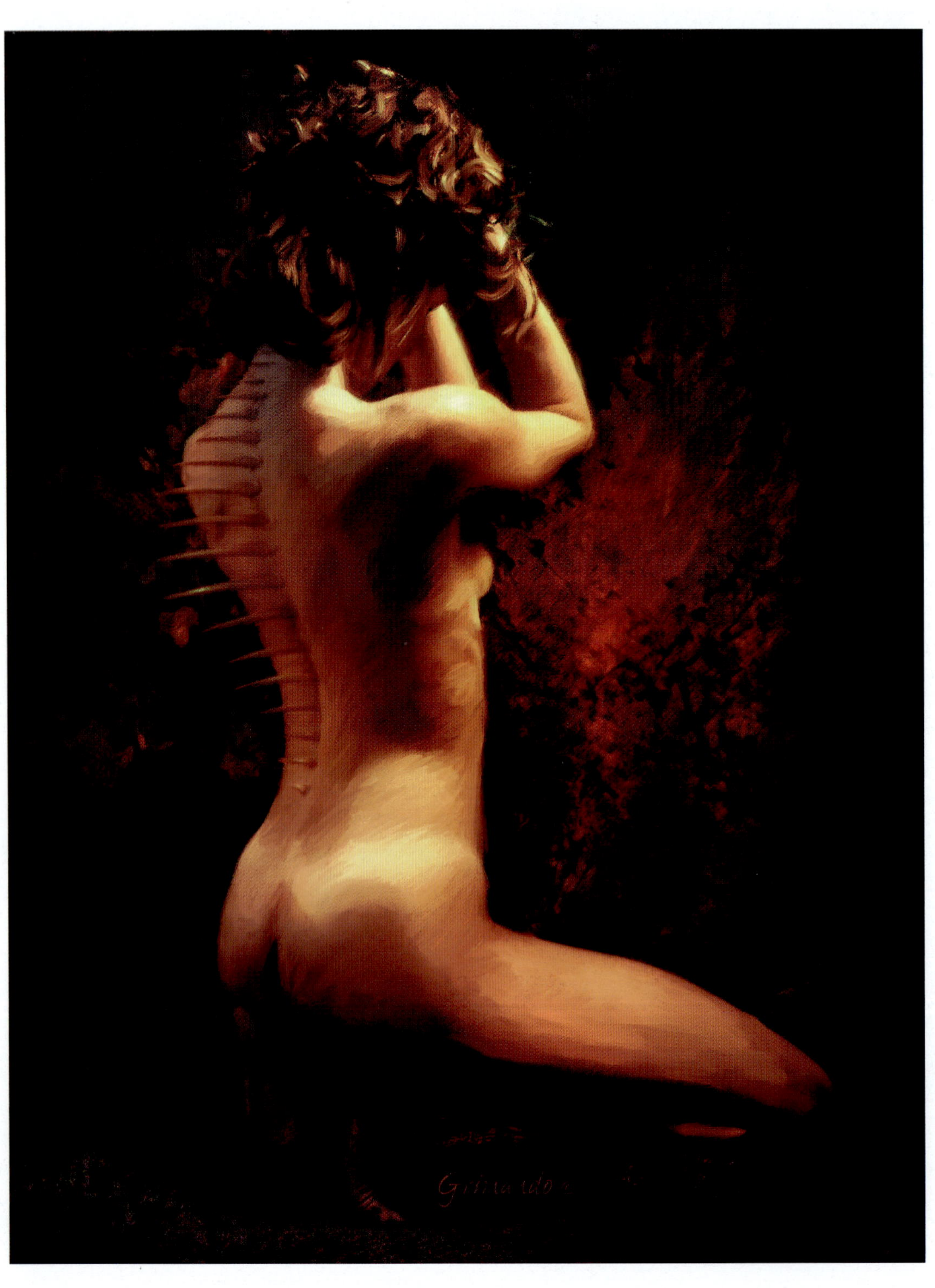

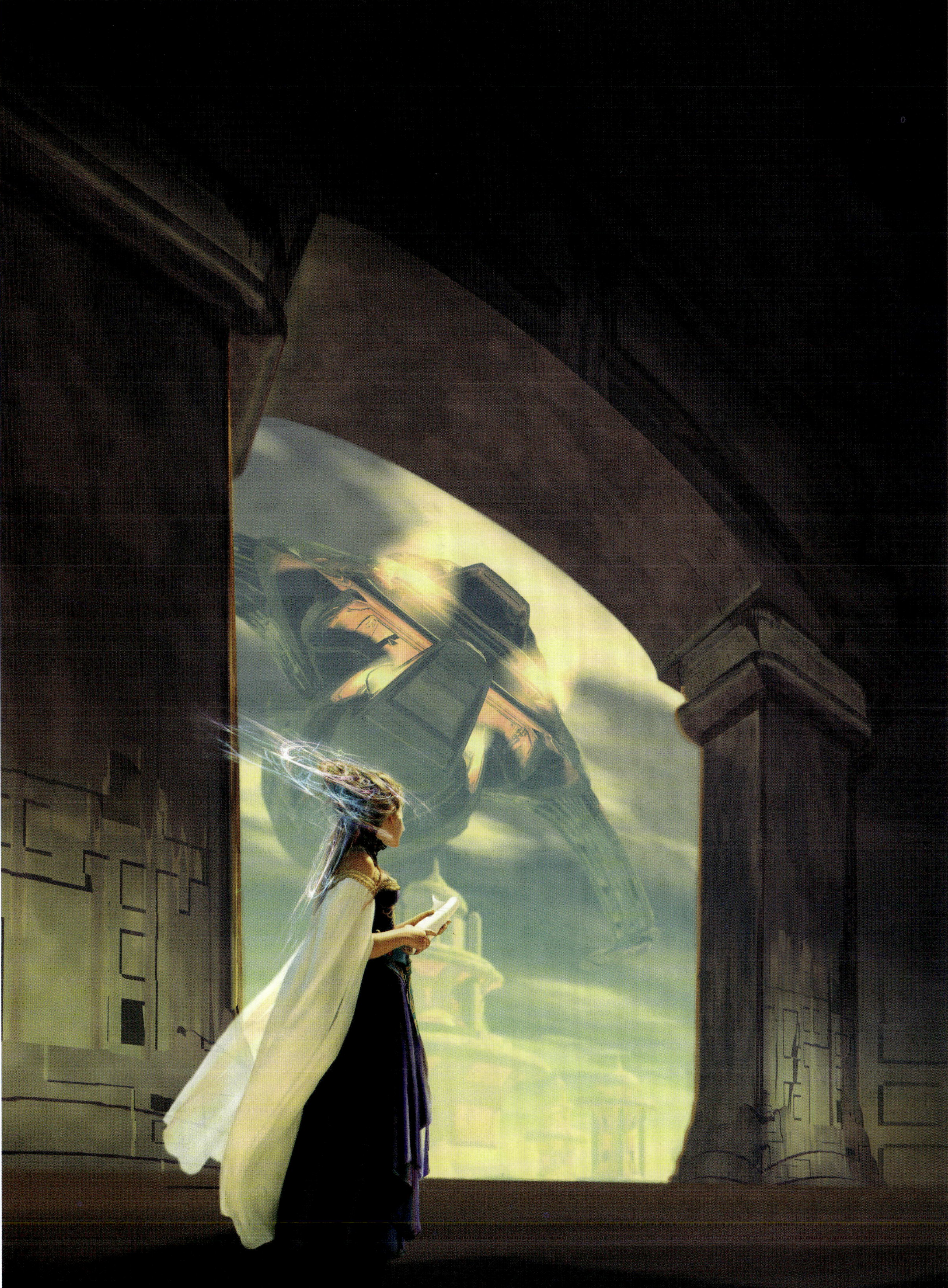

Journey's End

Digital: Photoshop

Perhaps the most symbolic of my recent work, Journey's End is like a lucid dream. The spirit is symbolized by the energy around the head and the figure is just about to leap into an unknown future after traveling along a dark tunnel.

This kind of work crosses the lines between photography and art. It makes a statement that couldn't be made by either one alone. That to me is what the digital revolution is all about, pushing the boundaries of art. Making new visual statements using the most contemporary tools.

Even galleries are beginning to accept multi-media as a viable contemporary art form. In some ways it overlaps the photographic art market since it can only be represented by reproductions but if an artist prints on watercolor paper as I do then he can make an original out of each print by enhancing it with pastels, watercolor, or any water based medium.

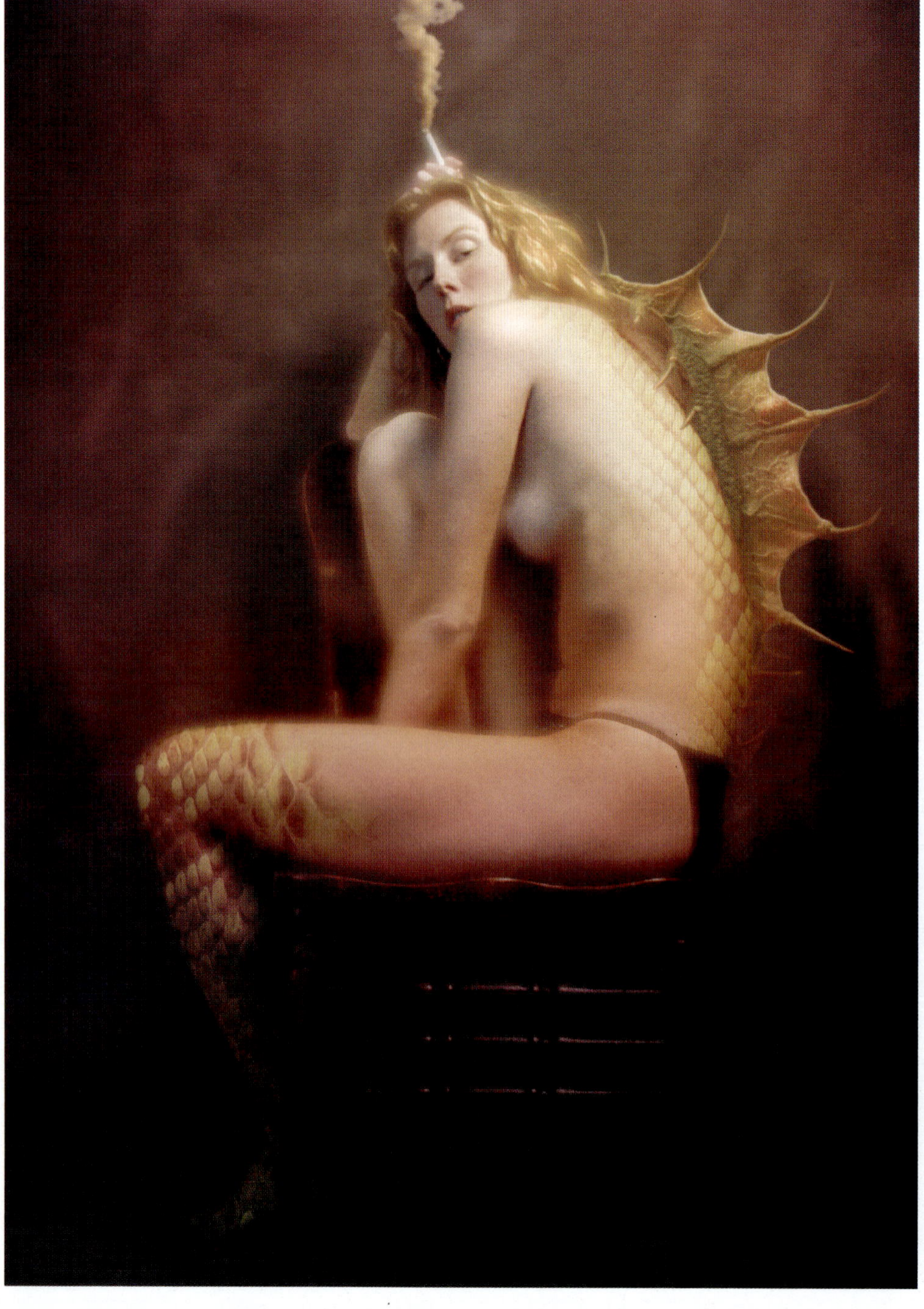

Spines 3

Digital: Photoshop/Painter

This is a not-so-subtle approach to my spines theme. I like the way the scales look like they could either be painted on or part of her skin. It begs the question, are the spines a part of her or a metaphor for our inner demons?

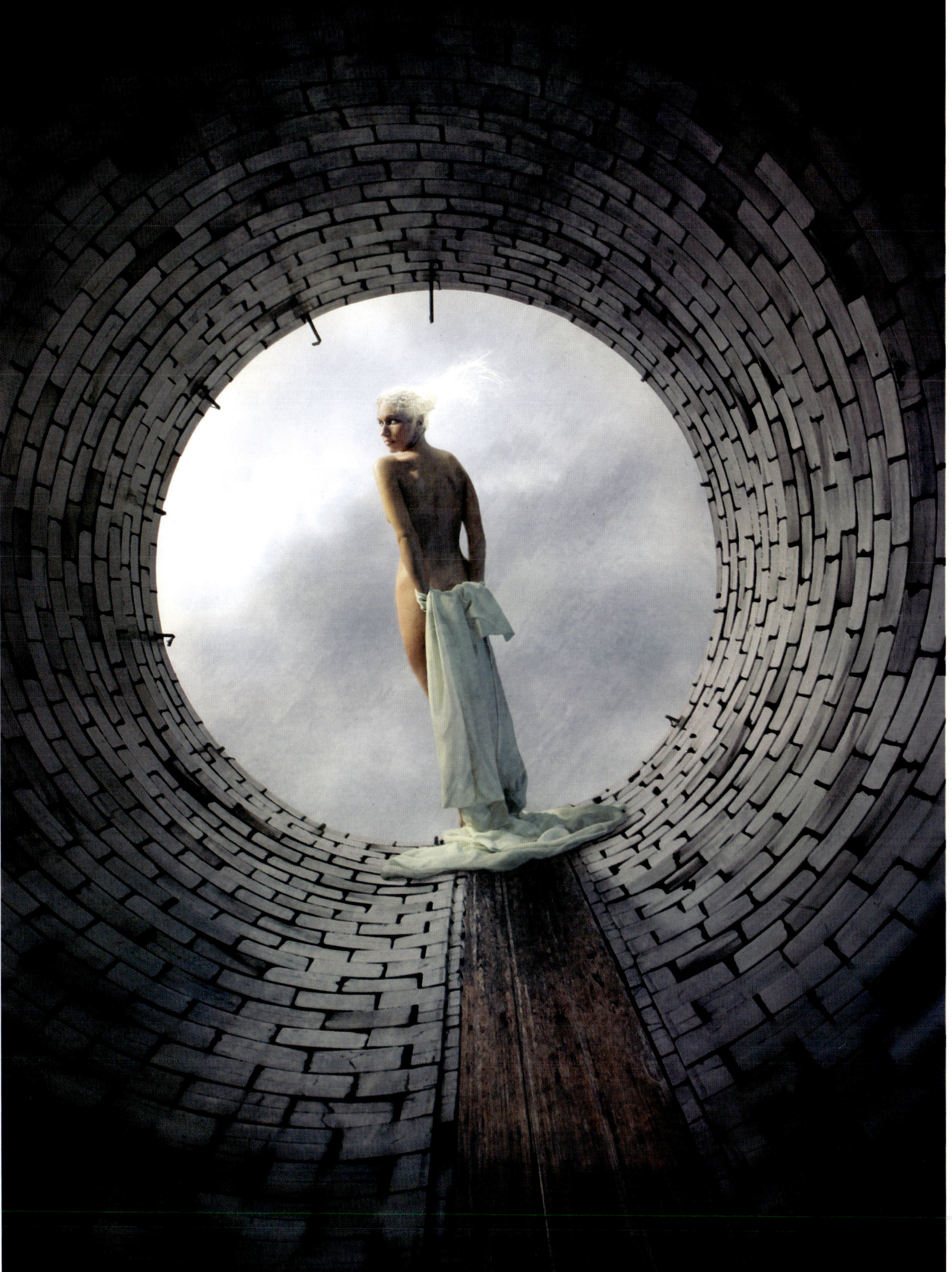

Bound

Digital: Photoshop

In “Bound” I use some of the same symbolism as “Journey’s End”. The spirit is represented as a flaming head and the hands are bound. Here, her clipped and broken wings accent the ruins. The mood is much different then “Journey’s End”, but I feel that it’s a hopeful piece because the flame (spirit) has not died out.

Since this new medium overlaps the photographic art world, I researched the best way to represent photography in high-end art galleries. I found that large limited edition C-Prints is the best way to showcase this kind of work.

The end result was a breathtaking 4’ x 6’ print that was near life size. This presentation makes you feel as though you can walk into the scene.

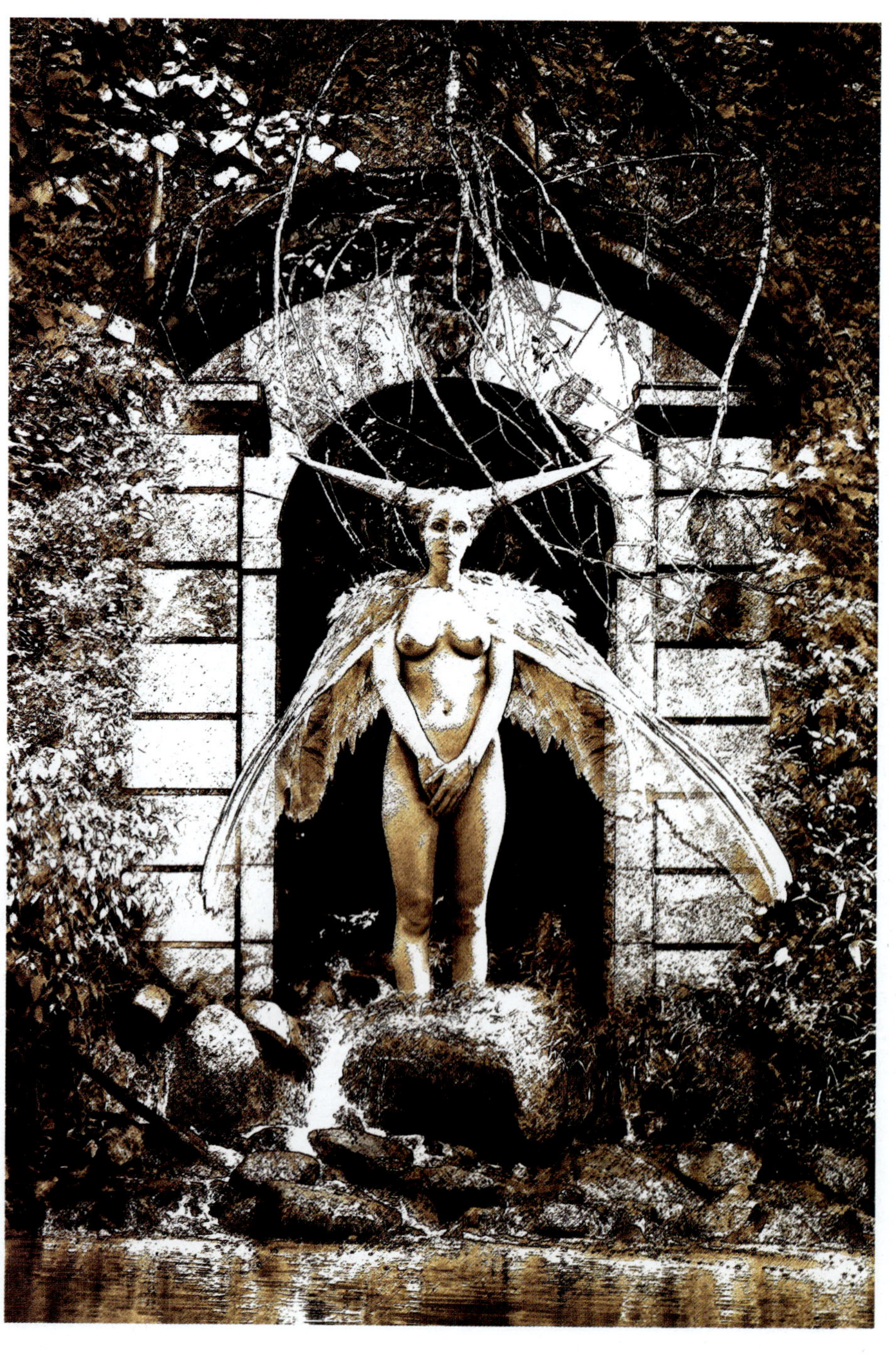

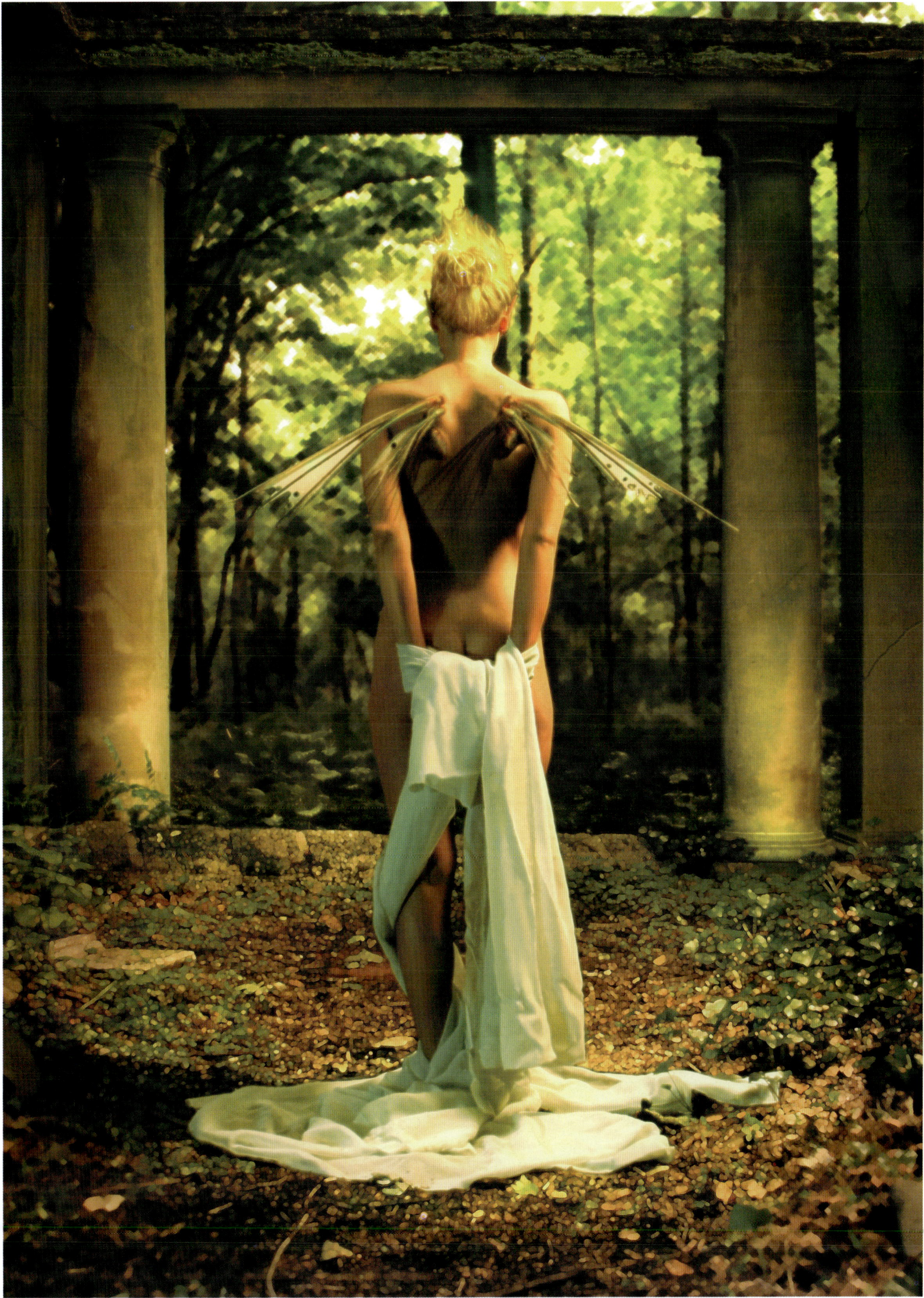

Robot Dreams

Digital: Photoshop/3D

This personal piece represents one of my favorite themes, the contrast between technology and nature. In this case, the robot represents technology. He dreams of princesses, fairies, dragons, and less complex times. It's symbolic of the artist's struggle with technology. Here I use the program Poser to create the robot and painstakingly model the rest of the scene in other 3D programs. Prior to computers the process was simpler but just as painstaking. By adapting to new ways of working I've been able to get much more creative. I've been able to strike a balance working both digitally and traditionally often crossing the lines between them. Sometimes though I long for the days of endless sketching and sitting at the easel.

Robot Dreams was used as a promotional piece for the progressive rock band, Paradox Engine and the cover of a Science Fiction Book Club catalog. It has a universal appeal. I've done a lot of work with Scott Goodman, the mind behind Paradox Engine. Scott and I even had a spoken word project called SG^2. My poetry backed by his music.

Atlantis

Digital: Photoshop/Painter/3D

The first CD cover for Paradox Engine

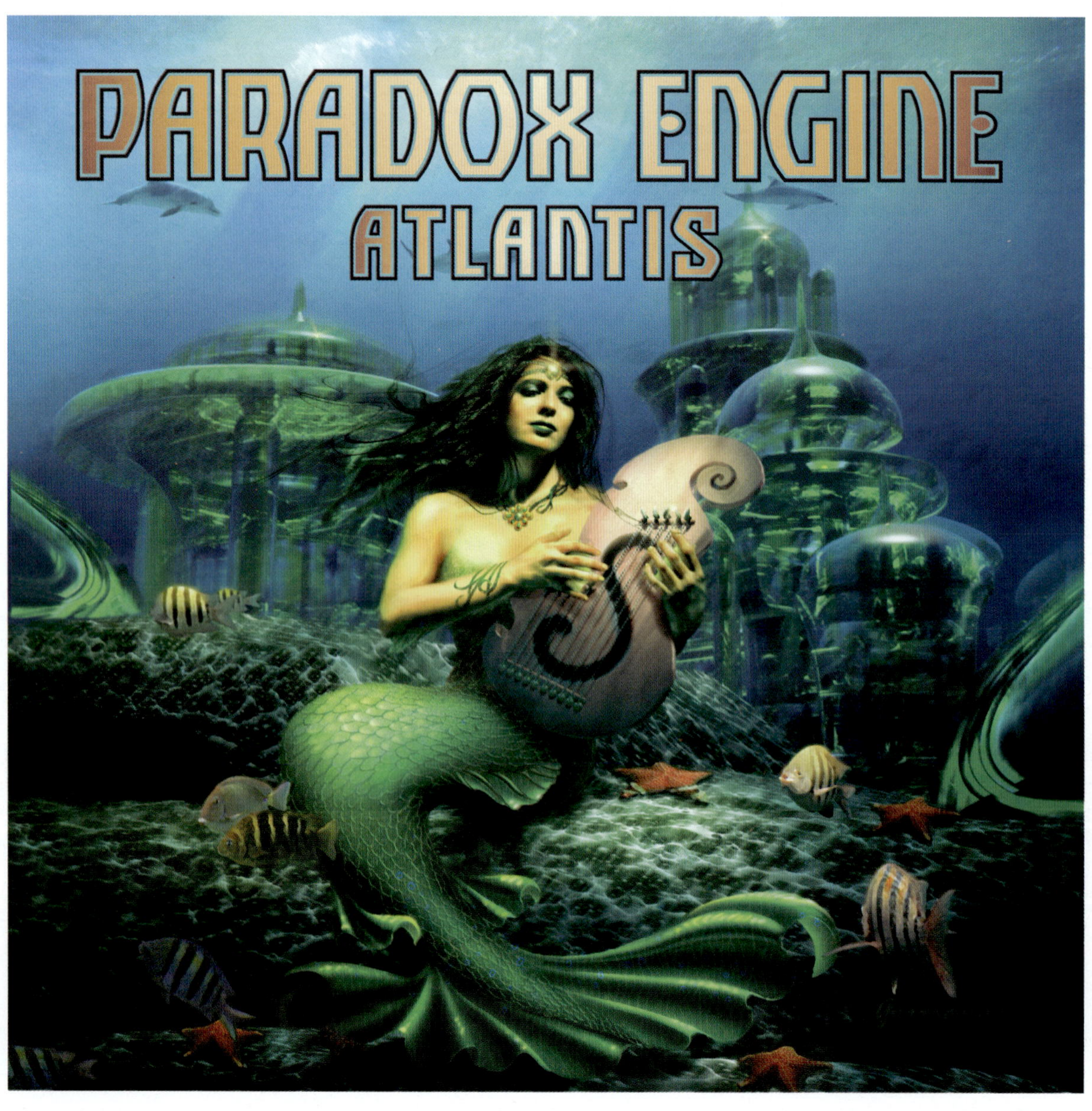

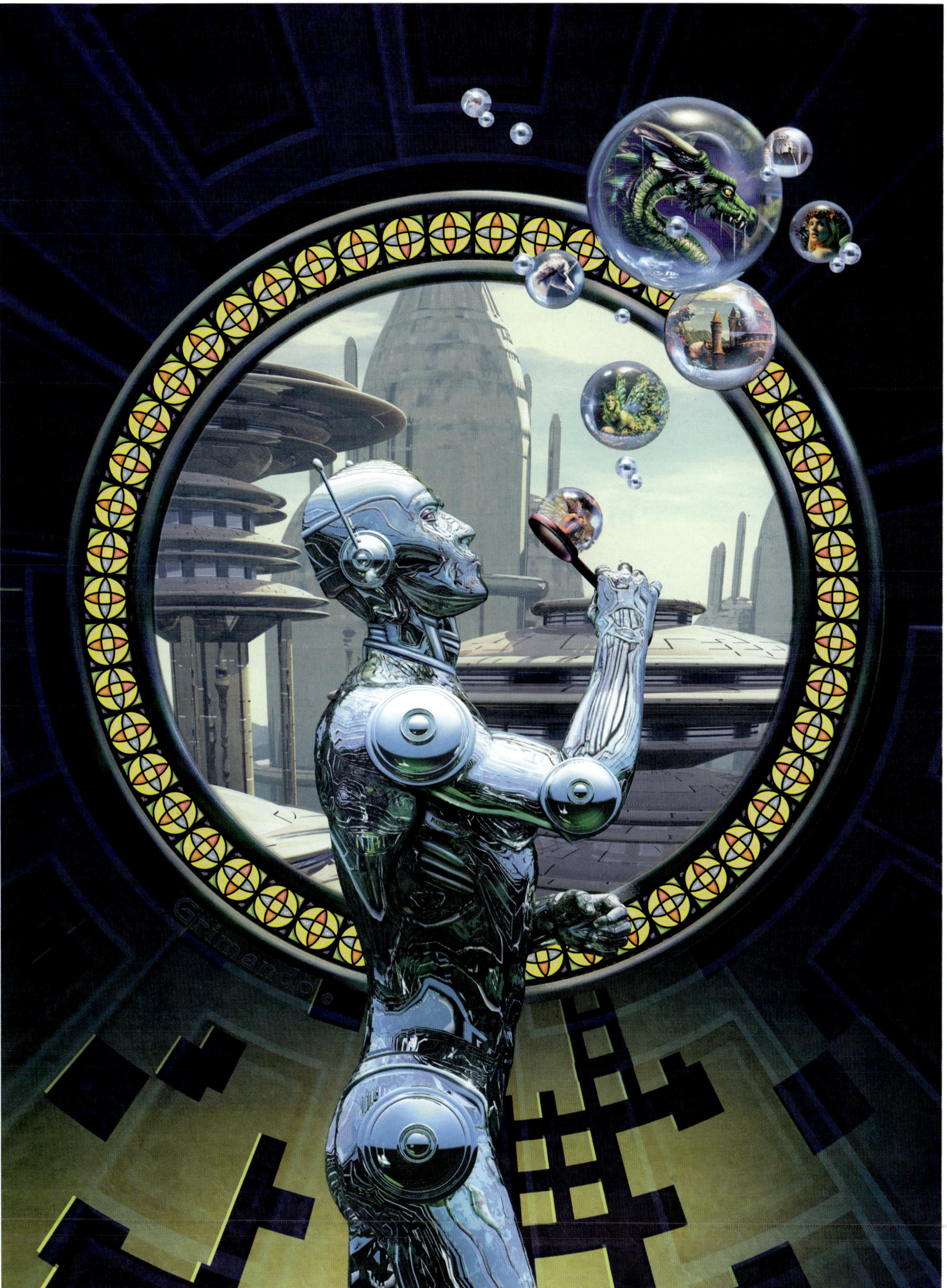
Grimando©

Morning Comes

Digital: Photoshop/Painter/Poser

This piece is an experiment I don't conduct to often. The advancements in the program Poser over the years has made it very easy to manipulate the pose and lighting on a reasonably good 3D model of a human being. Although I prefer to use Poser for preliminary comps and robot textures the temptation was too much in this case. The background reference has a difficult light source to duplicate in the studio. It was much easier to match the light and positioning in Poser. So I rendered it and brought it into Photoshop to blend it into the background and finished it in Painter. It's different but I kind of like the results.

Below is a sketch for an illustration I'm working on called, Chickadee.

In the next spread you'll find my short epic poem, The Dragon Slayer. I hope you enjoy it.

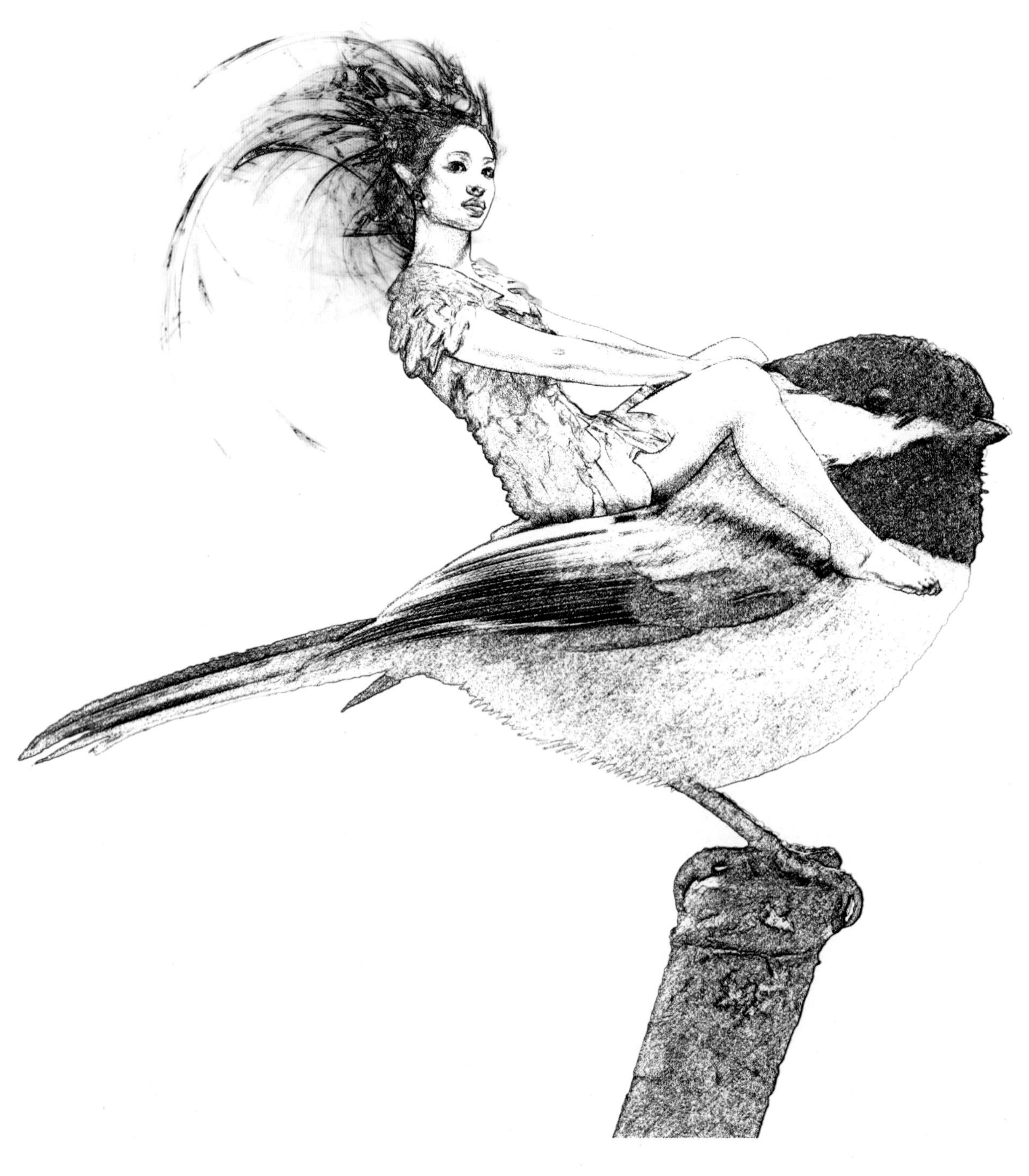

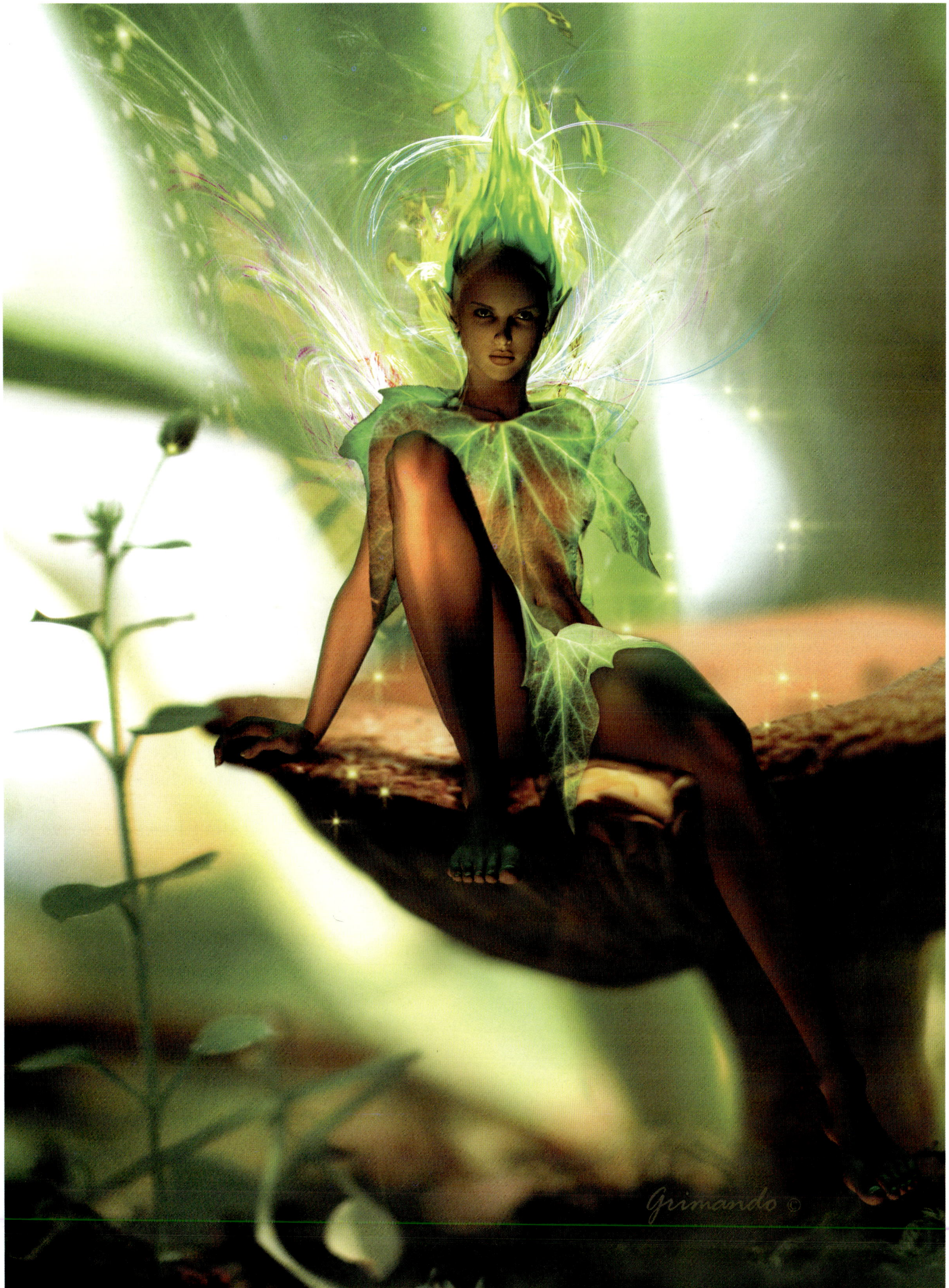
Grimando ©

The Dragon Slayer

by Scott Grimando

A Dragon Dwell In Mountain Caves
And On Moonlit Nights
Would Venture Out And
In His Hunger Make Men Slaves

His Will It Seemed Indomitable
For Men Are Dim & Slow
Though They Hasten To Their Doom
When Faced With Human Foe

Relying Then On Strength of Arms
Which Against His Brother
May Seem Strong
But Against A Dragon Do
Little Harm

The Dragon Was Quick
And Graceful And Cunning
The Sheep And The Cattle
Were His For The Culling

But Alone On A Hill
Lived A Worthy Foe
One That Men Rejected
In Spite Of Her Skill

Women Had No Right
To Bear Arms And Shield
There Was No Place For Them
On The Battlefield

But Born To Arms She Was
Raised By A Warrior
That Had No Son
Her Sword Arm Second To None

Determined To Prove It
She Donned Her Armor
A Thick Chest Plate
And the Helm of Her Father

She Sought Out The Beast
In Deep Mountain Caves
Where Men Feared To Chase
Else To Become A
Dragon's Feast

She Needn't Search Long
The Beast Had Smelled Her
A Mile Down Wind
And Rushed To Greet Her

She Noticed A Shadow
That Blocked Out The Sun
And Quickly Swung To Right
Narrowly Avoiding The Dragons Bite

The Beast Circled Around
On Strong Slender Wings
Surprised To See
A Slight Young Thing

If Dragons Had Whit
This One Would Have Snickered
At The Sight Of This Girl
With Hammered Armor To Fit

Despite Of Her Size
She Moved Like A Demon
Fast As A Blur
With Strong Able Thighs

Catching The Dragon Off Guard
She Leapt Off The Ground
Grazing His Wing With Sword
And Bringing Him Down

The Beast Did Tumble
And Rolled On Its Side
As The Lithe Able Warrior
Turned The Tides

Her Sword Cut A Gash
In The Dragons Tough Hide
Splattered With Blood
She Braced For The Kill

But The Dragon Was Far
From Done For Still
He Leapt To His Feet
Though He Could No Longer Fly

Racing Towards Her
With Reckless Abandon
Just As He Would
When Fighting A Man

But Fast As He Moved
She Was Faster
Dodging His Blow
And Striking Her Own

Her Sword Sunk Deep
A Killing Blow
Bringing The Dragon
Finally Down Low

So The Tales Still Speak
And People Still Praise Her
A Hero To All
The Dragon Slayer

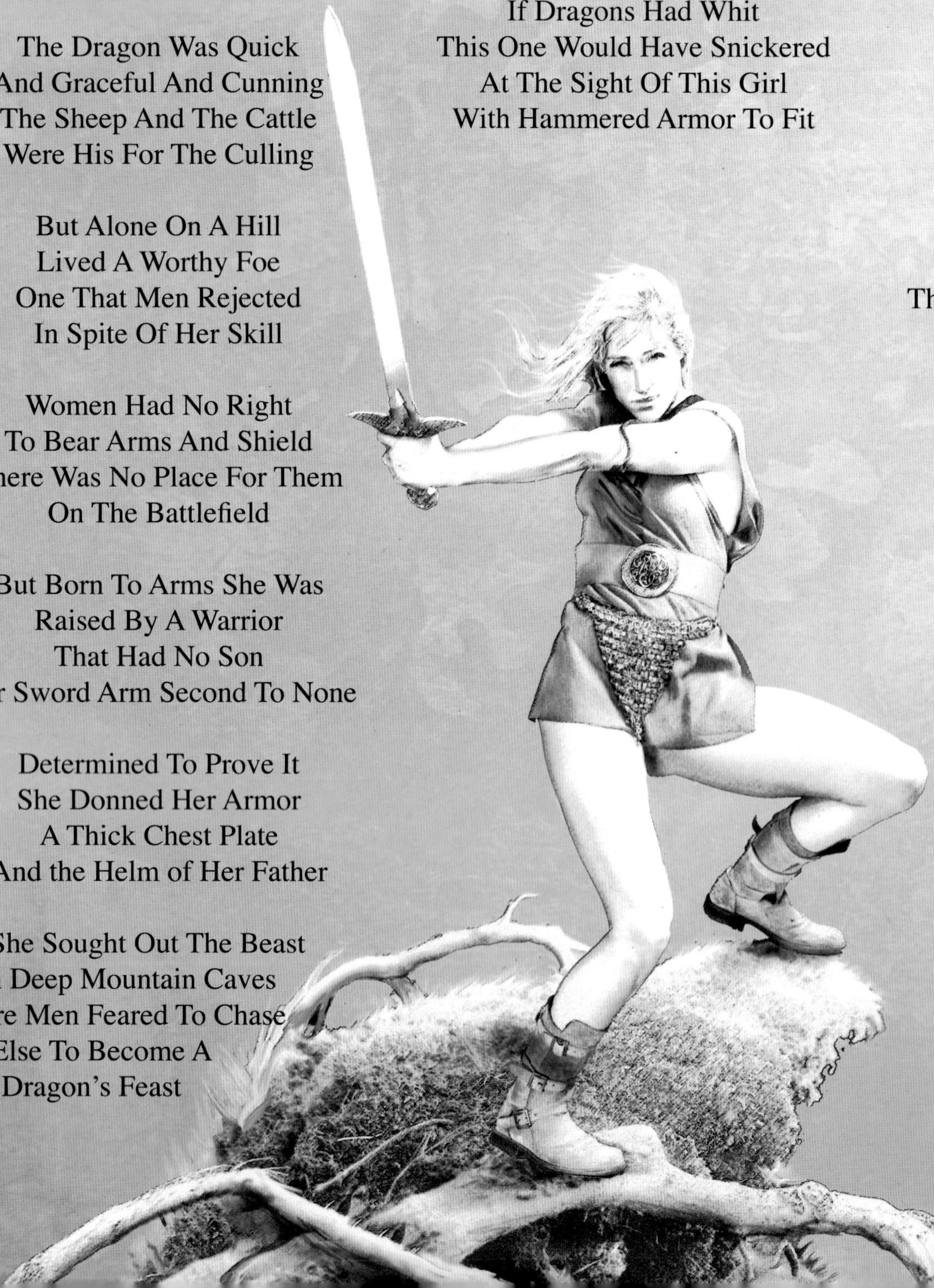

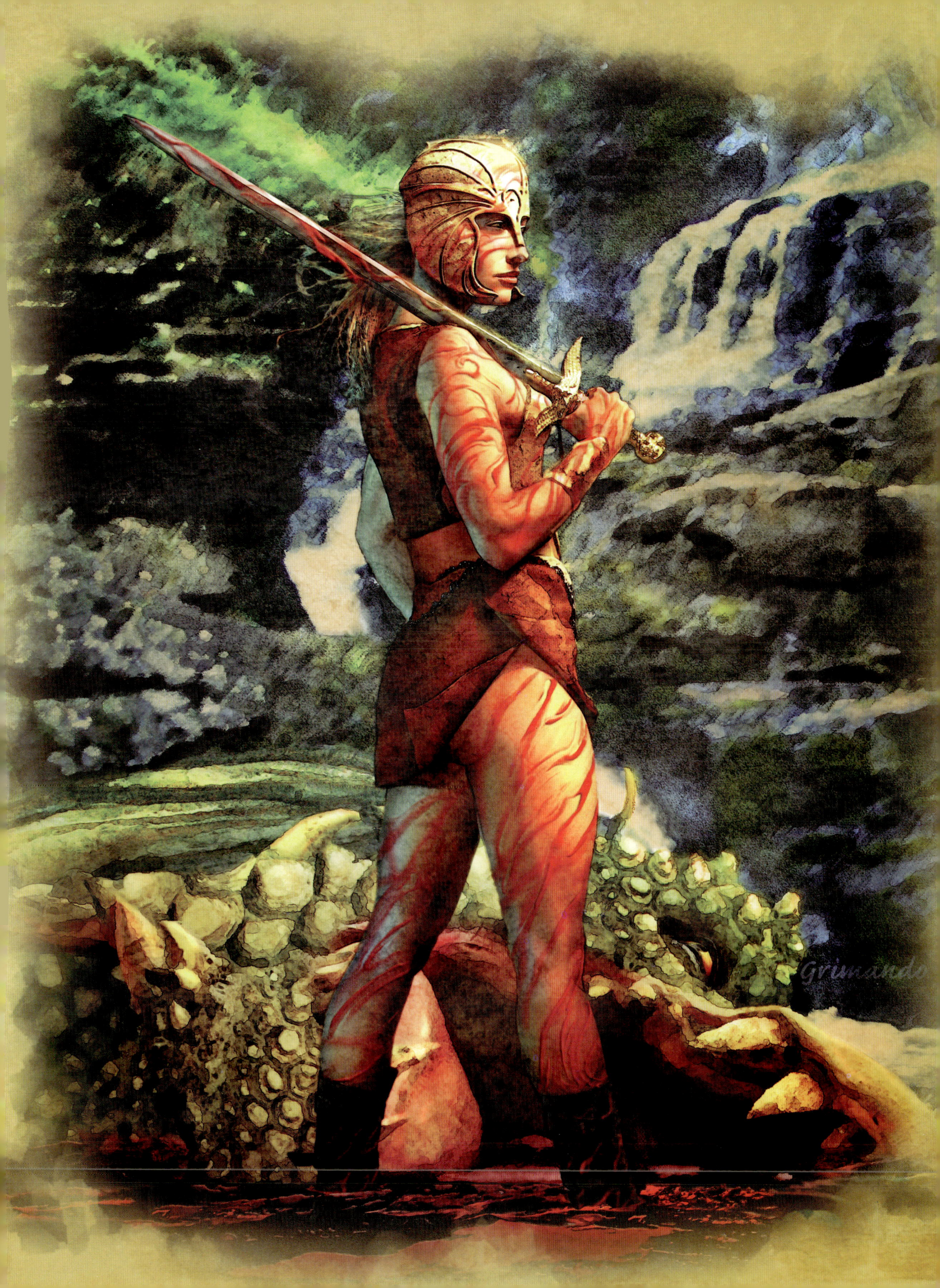
Grimando

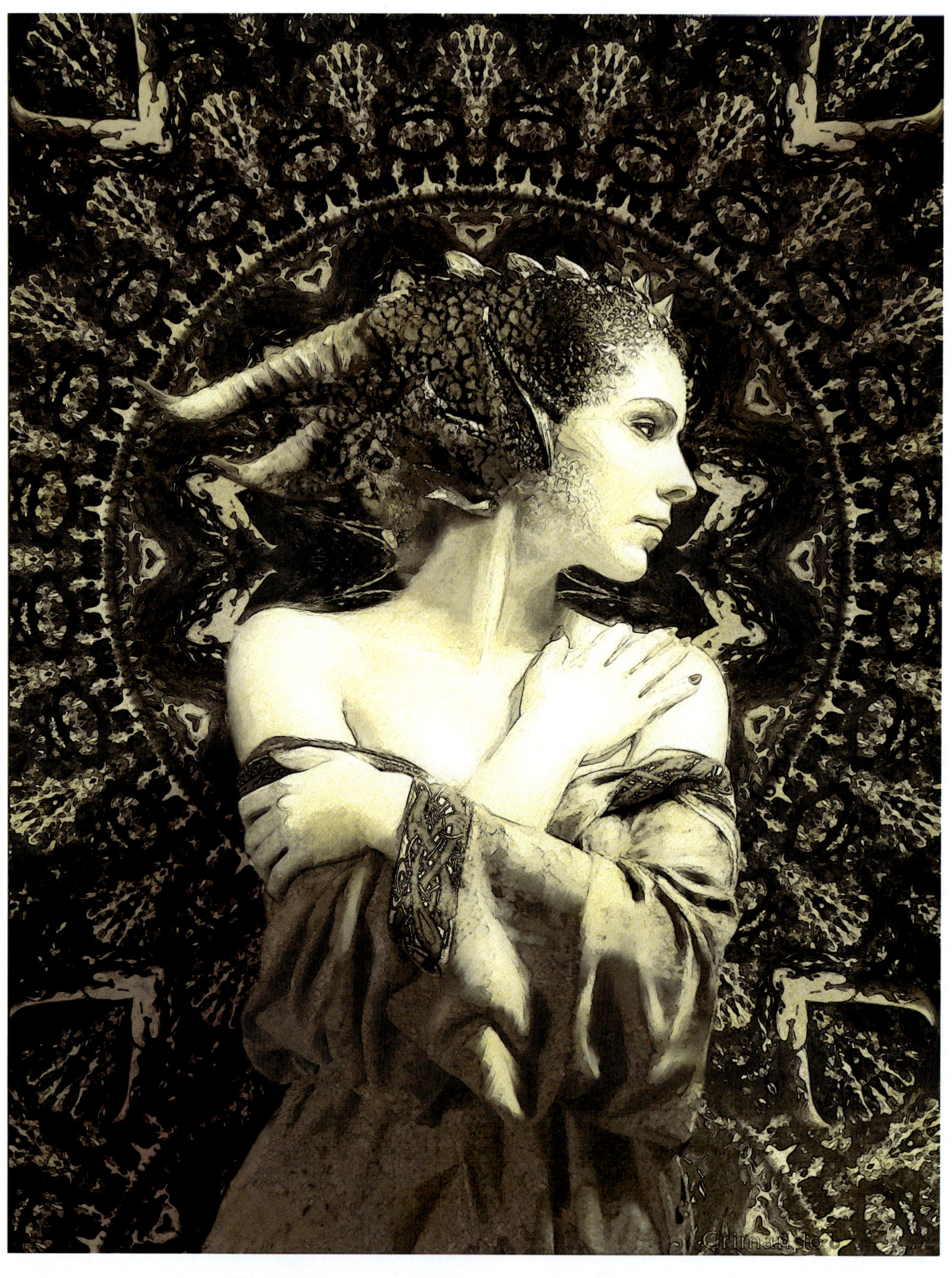

www.theArtoftheMyth.com

Is dedicated to the Art of the Mythical Woman.

www.GrimStudios.com

Is dedicated to everything else I do.